1|4|00

1995

P9-BXY-224

ALEXANDER GRAHAM BELL

Other titles in *Historical American Biographies*

Historical American Biographies

ALEXANDER GRAHAM BELL

Inventor and Teacher

Michael A. Schuman

Enslow Publishers, Inc.

44 Fadem Road   PO Box 38
Box 699   Aldershot
Springfield, NJ 07081   Hants GU12 6BP
USA   UK

http://www.enslow.com

Copyright © 1999 by Michael A. Schuman

All rights reserved.

No part of this book may be reproduced by any means
without the written permission of the publisher.

Library of Congress Cataloging-in-Publication Data

Schuman, Michael A.
   Alexander Graham Bell: inventor and teacher / Michael A. Schuman.
      p. cm. — (Historical American biographies)
   Includes bibliographical references and index.
   Summary: A biography of the man known for his interest in teaching
the deaf and for his invention of the telephone.
   ISBN 0-7660-1096-1
   1. Bell, Alexander Graham, 1847–1922—Juvenile literature.
   2. Inventors—United States—Biography—Juvenile literature. [1. Bell,
Alexander Graham, 1847–1922. 2. Inventors.] I. Title. II. Series.
TK6143.B4S38   1999
621.385'092—dc21
   [B]   98-14028
                                                        CIP
                                                        AC

Printed in the United States of America

10 9 8 7 6 5 4 3 2 1

To Our Readers:
All Internet addresses in this book were active and appropriate when we
went to press. Any comments or suggestions can be sent by e-mail to
Comments@enslow.com or to the address on the back cover.

Illustration Credits: Canadian Heritage-Parks Canada, Alexander
Graham Bell National Historic Site, Baddeck, Nova Scotia, pp. 8, 13,
24, 41, 44, 49, 54, 65, 79, 82, 87, 95, 98, 101, 106, 108, 113; Enslow
Publishers, Inc., pp. 26, 103; Gilbert H. Grosvenor Collection, Library
of Congress, pp. 21, 30, 56; Michael A. Schuman, p. 38; Reproduced
from the *Dictionary of American Portraits*, published by Dover
Publications, Inc., in 1967, p. 70.

Cover Illustration: © William B. Folsom 1986 (Background); Canadian
Heritage-Parks Canada, Alexander Graham Bell National Historic Site,
Baddeck, Nova Scotia (Inset).

Snyder County Library
Selinsgrove PA

CONTENTS

Acknowledgments

As usual, I would like to thank Charlotte Lesser and the staff at the Keene Public Library, as well as the staff at the library of Keene State College for their help. Many thanks for their time and assistance also go to Brian Wood at the Bell Homestead, Aynsley MacFarlane at Alexander Graham Bell National Historic Site, telephone historians Tom Hutchinson and Allen Koenigsberg, Rachel Merritt at the Mark Twain House, Linda Fry at the National Inventors Hall of Fame, Laura Jacobi at Gallaudet College, Tom Crouch at the Smithsonian Institution, Len Bruno at the Library of Congress, and Douglas Tarr at Edison National Historic Site.

Alexander Graham Bell

1

"I HEAR!
I HEAR!"

Alexander Graham Bell never wanted to make the trip to Philadelphia. Yet there he was.

Bell was a full-time teacher at Boston University in Massachusetts. As a second job, he tutored deaf children. In his spare time he worked on inventing machines. One was a device many thought was impossible. It would be able to transmit the human voice over a wire. Bell called it a telephone.

The year was 1876, the one-hundredth anniversary of the American Declaration of Independence. Celebrations were taking place all over the United States. The biggest of all was the world's fair in Philadelphia.

World's fairs were once major events. They took place every few years in different nations. People traveled from all over the world to attend them. At the fairs were pavilions showing both the cultures of different countries and new inventions.

The 1876 world's fair in Philadelphia was officially called the Centennial Exhibition. One of the many pavilions was devoted to electrical inventions. Yet Bell had no interest in showing off his invention at the world's fair.[1] The fair opened in the spring— a hectic time at the university. Bell had students' tests to grade.

There may have been other reasons Bell did not want to present his telephone at the fair. Perhaps he was afraid that it would not work properly, and he would be embarrassed. Maybe he thought it needed more work.

World's Fairs

World's fairs have introduced people to inventions ranging from the Ferris wheel to television. As recently as the 1960s, world's fairs in New York City and Montreal were hugely popular events. Critics have said that today's many theme parks have made world's fairs unnecessary. However, there was a world's fair in 1998 in Lisbon, Portugal.

Bell's fiancée, Mabel Hubbard, and her father, Gardiner Hubbard, were eager for Bell to show off the telephone. Mabel, who was deaf, had been one of Bell's students. To her and her father, the world's fair seemed to be the chance of a lifetime for Bell. Newspaper reporters and scientists from all over the world would be there. Judges would present awards to the best and most promising inventions.

Still, Bell refused to go.

Then he learned that he had missed the deadline to apply for a space in the electrical inventions pavilion. To Bell's relief, it seemed the matter was finished. However, Gardiner Hubbard, a respected lawyer, was on a committee responsible for the world's fair exhibit devoted to the state of Massachusetts. He arranged for Bell to demonstrate his telephone in that pavilion instead of the one for electrical inventions.

June 24 started out as a typical day for Bell. He was hard at work at the university. Mabel surprised him by arranging an afternoon carriage ride for just the two of them. For Bell it was a chance to briefly leave the pressures of work.

To the Train Station

What Bell did not know was that Mabel had planned for the coach driver to take them to the train station. Mabel had secretly bought Bell a round-trip ticket to Philadelphia. She and her mother had packed his suitcase the night before and had hidden it in the carriage.

It did not matter. When they arrived at the station, Bell refused to board the train.

Although Mabel could not hear, she was able to speak in a limited way. She read lips and had been taught to pronounce sounds. Mabel began crying and said, "If—if you don't love me enough to do this for me, I—I won't marry you!"[2]

Bell boarded the train.

En route to Philadelphia, Bell wrote a letter home. It read,

Dear Mabel,

There's no turning back now. I shall be in Philadelphia tonight. I must confess, however, I don't see what good I can accomplish there.

Alec[3]

Bell and his telephone were given a remote position in the Massachusetts pavilion. His invention was to be judged on Sunday, June 25, a day when the fair was closed to the public.

That Sunday dawned brutally hot. Local newspapers had said Philadelphians were suffering "the hottest summer in eighty years."[4] June 25 was one of the hottest days of that summer.

Air-conditioning had not been invented yet, and it was unheard of for people to appear in public wearing shorts or short-sleeved shirts. People dressed in clothing that covered them from neck to

Alexander Graham Bell used this pass to enter the Centennial Exhibition, where he first showed his telephone to the world in 1876.

feet. Bell hated the brutal heat and humidity.[5] It gave him piercing headaches.

Bell was not the only person who felt sick from the heat. Visitors became ill with what was called Centennial Fever. Even the judges could barely stand it. They were so sweaty and tired that they decided to quit early on June 25. They would continue judging exhibits another day.

However, Bell had to return to Boston the next day to give tests to his students. It seemed that the entire trip had been a waste.

The Emperor Arrives

Suddenly Bell was spotted by a bearded, stocky man he had met before. The man was Emperor Pedro II of Brazil, also known as Dom Pedro. Dom Pedro had visited Bell on a trip to Boston. There, the two men had spent time discussing methods of teaching the hearing-impaired.

When Dom Pedro spotted Bell at the exhibition, he cried out, "I think it is Mr. Bell. This is a far distance from your classes. How are the deaf-mutes of Boston?"[6]

Dom Pedro and Bell chatted for a while. Then Dom Pedro, who was one of the exhibition judges, asked to see Bell's invention.

The teacher from Boston led Dom Pedro to the telephone receiver. Bell then sat at the transmitter five hundred feet away and began reciting a speech from Shakespeare's play *Hamlet*. Dom Pedro was stunned. His eyes lit up. "I hear! I hear!" he called out.[7]

Other judges rushed to hear the amazing talking machine. For the next three hours, they ignored the heat and humidity to examine the gadget. Among the judges was a respected English scientist named Sir William Thomson. Thomson exclaimed to the other judges, "Gentlemen, this is the most wonderful thing I have seen in America."[8]

Bell returned to Boston the next day. In December he learned that he had been given a great honor—a Centennial Exhibition award for his telephone.

2

GHOSTS AND MACHINES

Although Bell worked in Boston, he was not born there. In fact, he was not a native of the United States. Alexander Bell was born on March 3, 1847, in Edinburgh, Scotland. At birth he had no middle name. He was just Alexander Bell.

The Bell family was comfortable, though not rich. The baby's grandfather, also named Alexander Bell, was a part-time actor and teacher. He taught about proper speaking and speech difficulties.

The boy's father, Alexander Melville Bell, was also a speech teacher. He was so excited about the subject that he spent his free time researching the mechanics of speech. He devoted many hours to exploring how people spoke and what parts of the mouth made certain sounds.

Alexander's mother, Eliza Symonds Bell, was hearing-impaired. She could hear only by using a rubber ear tube, a device shaped like a horn that she placed near her ear. People who wanted to say something to her would speak directly into the ear tube.

Alexander Melville and Eliza Bell had a son named Melville James Bell in 1845. He was called Melly. Alexander was born two years later. In 1848, the Bells' last child, Edward Charles Bell, was born.

Young Alexander spent his childhood years in Edinburgh. Today, Edinburgh is best known as a favorite stop for tourists. They love to walk down the handsomely landscaped street known as the Royal Mile. They spend time exploring the city's museums, Edinburgh Castle, and the lavish Palace of Holyroodhouse. In the 1500s, Holyroodhouse had been the home of Mary Queen of Scots and other members of royalty.

When Alexander was a boy, Edinburgh was not a tourist center. It was the political capital of Scotland. It was also one of the many factory cities in Great Britain. Like most other industrial cities, it was noisy, smelly, and crowded.

Aleck, as he was called, never liked city life. Even as a boy, he preferred open spaces. His earliest memory was of a family visit to a spot called Ferny

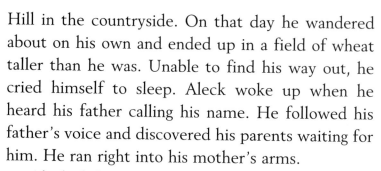

The Scottish Heritage

The people of Scotland have an ancient past. Around the year A.D. 600, four tribal groups—the Scots, the Picts, the Britons, and the Angles—joined to fight a common enemy, the Norsemen. Their first king, Malcolm III, was chosen in 1057. The events leading up to his reign were later immortalized by Shakespeare in his classic play *Macbeth*.

Hill in the countryside. On that day he wandered about on his own and ended up in a field of wheat taller than he was. Unable to find his way out, he cried himself to sleep. Aleck woke up when he heard his father calling his name. He followed his father's voice and discovered his parents waiting for him. He ran right into his mother's arms.

Aleck did not attend school as a child. He was taught at home by his mother. Although he was not in daily contact with other schoolchildren, he still caught serious illnesses. Vaccinations like those we have today did not exist. It was common for children under the age of ten to die from some of these diseases.

One dangerous childhood illness was scarlet fever. It is caused by bacteria and produces a high fever and a scarlet rash. The fever would sometimes cause children's minds to play tricks on them.

Aleck was lying in bed suffering from scarlet fever when he was sure he saw a ghost. It stood at the foot of his bed and wore a long cloak. It did not make a sound. At first, Aleck was frightened. He continued to stare at it. However, it never moved or made a noise. Finally, Aleck mustered up the courage to approach it. He pulled at the cloak and dragged it into bed.

Aleck later wrote, "This did not better matters, however, for now I saw the ghostly figure lying near me on the bed staring at me with shadowy eyes. I could stand the strain no longer and, thoroughly alarmed, I screamed for help."[1]

It turned out that the scary ghost was only his mother's cloak and cap, which she had hung on his bedpost.

A Curious Boy

By the time he was four, Aleck showed an interest in words and language. Once, his interest got him into trouble. The Bells had a family friend staying overnight in their home. Like many children, Aleck was curious. He sneaked inside the guest's bedroom and saw stationery and an inkwell.

Aleck used the paper and ink without the guest's permission. He wanted to write a "letter." He scribbled on the paper and put it in an envelope. He then made more scribbles on the envelope, which became the "address." He took one of the guest's postage stamps and put it on the envelope. He asked one of his family's young servants for a place to mail the letter. She found the whole thing amusing and laughed.

Aleck was then called into his father's office. He was asked where he got the stamp. Aleck was scared. He lied and said that his mother had gotten it for him. Then Alexander Melville asked Aleck to go get his mother. Instead Aleck ran to a guest room and hid behind a dresser. His parents looked and looked but could not find him. Aleck continued hiding throughout the evening and missed dinner.

By then his parents were worried. They thought the boy might have run away. They decided to look one more time in the house before calling the police. Sure enough, they found him behind the dresser. He was punished with a spanking from his father.

As Aleck grew up, his father became well known as a teacher of those who had trouble hearing or speaking. Alexander Melville Bell spent time writing books on the subject. He was working hard on a "visible speech," or "universal alphabet," project. This alphabet would have a symbol for every sound the human voice is capable of making, including grunts, coughs, and growls. The task was enormous.

While his father was busy with his work, Aleck continued with his home schooling. When he was ten years old, his mother decided she had taught him as much as she could. It was time for him to learn in a more formal setting. In 1857 Aleck and his younger brother, Edward (known as Ted), began classes at a private school called Hamilton Place Academy.

Aleck was not much of a student. His grades were fair. He was more interested in doing experiments and discovering things on his own. He was so independent that he gave himself a new name at age ten. He felt there had been too many other "Alexander Bells" in his family.[2] The name did not seem to be anything special.

He later wrote, "Alexander Bell was not nearly substantial enough to suit me. So I chose the surname of one of my father's former pupils, who had come to board at our house, Alexander Graham. It had a fine strong sound to it."[3]

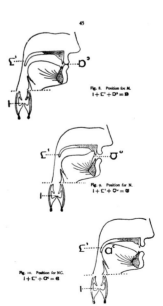

First Invention

When Aleck was eleven years old, a boy named

Alexander Melville Bell drew these diagrams as part of his work on the visible speech system.

Ben Herdman became a student of Bell's father. Aleck and Ben were the same age and became good friends.

One day Aleck and Ben were horsing around in a flour mill that Ben's father owned. They were annoying Mr. Herdman, who told them to go do something constructive. Aleck replied rudely by asking Mr. Herdman to name something that would be constructive. Herdman told them to find a way to take husks off wheat.

The boys took him seriously. They went and found a rotating machine once used at the mill. Aleck came up with the idea of putting paddles with nails on the rotating machine. As the machine turned, the nails tore the husks off the wheat.

Bell later said, "It was a proud day for us when we boys marched into Mr. Herdman's office, presented him with our sample of cleaned wheat, and suggested paddling wheat in a dried-out vat."[4]

Herdman was impressed. He used the boys' invention in his mill. Bell later wrote that Herdman's command to do something useful was his first motivation for inventing.

A Budding Poet

Yet Bell was inventive in other ways, too. Alexander Melville Bell bought a second home outside Edinburgh when Aleck was eleven. Aleck liked writing poetry in the garden of the new family home. He surrounded himself with the beauty of nature and wrote about sunny days and the outdoors.

When he was thirteen, Aleck wrote a special poem for his grandfather, Alexander Bell. Grandfather Bell was living far away in London and had just turned seventy. Aleck admired his grandfather. He was especially taken with the fact that both grandfather and grandson shared the same birthday, March 3. Aleck wrote:

> *I am thirteen years old I find,*
> *Your birthday and mine are the same.*
> *I wish to inherit your mind,*
> *As well as your much honoured name.*[5]

Aleck also loved science. He and some friends formed a club and gave it a scholarly name: The Society for the Promotion of Fine Arts among Boys. Each boy was given the title of "professor" of a topic. Aleck was professor of anatomy. In his room at home he kept birds' eggs and animal skeletons. He had no interest in killing animals for the sake of science. However, he would dissect those he found already dead.

Aleck graduated from Hamilton Place Academy and went to public high school. Royal High School was located on a commanding spot, high on a hill with a wonderful view of historic Edinburgh Castle. In his second year at the school, Aleck and his classmates played the English game of cricket at Holyrood Park, not far from the spot where Mary Queen of Scots once ruled.

The Bell family sat for this photograph while they lived in Scotland. Left to right are Aleck, Melville (Melly), and Edward (Ted), standing behind their parents Eliza and Alexander Melville Bell.

Entering his teenage years, Aleck was a handsome boy. He was tall and slender and had coal black wavy hair parted on the side. Still, he was only an average student. He hated learning classical languages such as Latin and Greek.[6] He was even bored with subjects he enjoyed, such as mathematics.[7] His older brother, Melly, had won class honors in high school. Aleck won nothing.

Moving to London

When Aleck was fifteen, his father decided he might become more mature if he lived with his grandfather. So in 1862, Aleck took the train and traveled roughly 330 miles south to London.

Soon after he arrived, Grandfather Bell bought Aleck a whole new wardrobe. He said that casual clothes that were appropriate in the small city of Edinburgh would not do in a world capital like London. One time when Aleck was dressed in his best new clothes, a man hauling a cart tipped his hat to him as a sign of respect. Aleck learned that if you looked important, people treated you as if you were important.

Still, sharp clothes did not mean a sharp mind. Aleck's grandfather quickly realized that the boy was not interested in learning standard lessons. Instead, he invited some of his educated and accomplished friends to his house. They would discuss the latest mechanical inventions or developments in medicine. The older man encouraged Aleck to participate in the discussions.

Milton and Shakespeare

Grandfather Bell gave Aleck some of the great works of literature to read. These included the epic poems of John Milton and the plays of William Shakespeare. Grandfather and grandson discussed them together. Grandfather Bell took Aleck to the theater so he could study the art of acting. Aleck was so impressed that he considered becoming an actor. But his grandfather discouraged him. Acting was not considered a respectable profession at that

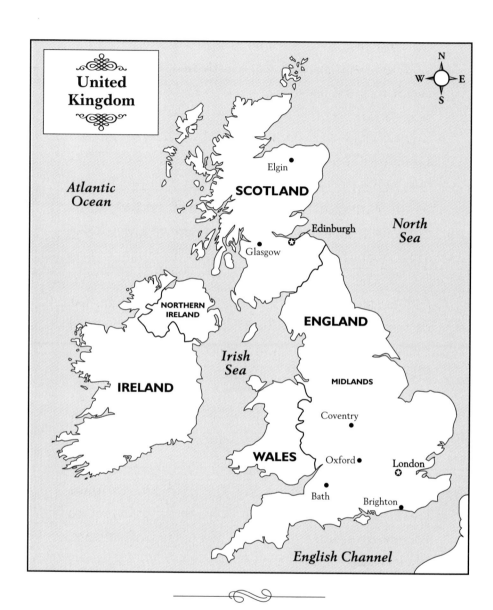

Alexander Graham Bell was born in Edinburgh, Scotland. As a young man, he lived for a time with his grandfather in London, England.

time. Also, like now, it was a hard field in which to earn a living.

Aleck enjoyed his time with his grandfather so much that he asked his parents if he could stay a few months longer. They agreed. When the time was up, Alexander Melville Bell took the train to London to bring Aleck home. The father found that his son had matured greatly in just one year. Aleck later wrote that the time he spent with his grandfather in London "converted me from a boy somewhat prematurely into a man."[8]

On their way back home to Edinburgh, father and son stopped to visit a respected British scientist named Sir Charles Wheatstone. Wheatstone had made a speaking machine based on the notes of a German scientist who had lived one hundred years earlier. By turning two cranks, Wheatstone's machine imitated the sound of the human voice. It could even "speak" a full sentence.

When the Bells returned to Edinburgh, the father challenged sons Melly and Aleck to make their own talking machine. The teenagers went to the local butcher and were given a lamb's throat. They studied it and then made their own fake larynx (the tube that contains vocal chords) from tin and rubber.

Then they asked a neighborhood pharmacist if they could borrow a human skull. With that model, they built their own mouth and lower jaw with a hard rubbery substance called gutta-percha. They used a bellows to blow air into the mouth. With a little work, the Bell boys' talking machine made a sound like a baby saying "Mama, mama." It sounded so much like a baby that people living in their apartment building thought it was a real one. The boys had good laughs playing tricks on their neighbors with their talking machine.

Experiments aside, Aleck believed his father did not treat him like an adult, as his grandfather did. He wanted to leave home. He actually considered running away and becoming a sailor. Instead, he applied for a job as a teacher in a school called Weston House. It was located in Elgin, a small Scottish fishing town. Bell got the job.

At age sixteen, this boy who had been only a fair student was going to be a teacher. Some of his students would be older than he was!

3

ACROSS THE WATERS

Alexander Graham Bell stood tall and in command of his students. He had no trouble taking charge of his class. It did not matter that he was only sixteen years old.

Teaching kept him busy. At his most stressful times, Bell suffered from painful headaches. During very busy periods, he often had trouble clearing his mind at the end of the day, which caused him to have difficulty sleeping.

As before, Bell enjoyed escaping to the country-side to relax. In small seaside Elgin, a quiet restful spot was never far away. One of Bell's favorite places was a little hill called Lady Mound. He liked to relax by stretching out on the grass and watching the seagulls.

When the school year was finished, Bell returned to Edinburgh. The year was 1864. Across the ocean, the United States was in the middle of its brutal Civil War. Yet in the Bell family home in Scotland, the biggest news was Aleck's father's success. Alexander Melville Bell had finally completed his visible speech alphabet. It included a total of thirty-four symbols.

His next step was to show people that this new alphabet really worked. In 1864 there were few of the technological wonders we have today. There was no computer, television, or radio. And, of course, there was no telephone. There were newspapers, but the best way to spread news of a new invention or creation was to demonstrate it to a live audience.

The Bell family visited universities, where

Alexander Melville Bell finally completed his system of visible speech for the hearing-impaired in 1864. This chart shows the symbols used to represent the sounds of the human voice in his system.

Alexander Melville Bell spoke before audiences of professors and scientists. Sons Melly and Aleck would go with him, but they would stay out of hearing range.

The father would ask people in the audience to make noises. They could be real words, nonsense words, laughs, groans, or any other kind of sound. He would then write his symbol for each noise on a chalkboard.

Alexander Graham Bell remembered,

> I was then called in, and the symbols were presented to me to interpret; and I could read in each symbol a direction to do something with my mouth.
>
> I remember upon one occasion the attempt to follow directions resulted in a curious rasping noise that was utterly unintelligible to me. The audience, however, at once responded with loud applause. They recognized it as an imitation of the noise of sawing wood, which had been given by an amateur ventriloquist as a test.[1]

Word got out about this teacher and his new universal alphabet. Even those who had trouble believing it could work changed their minds after seeing it demonstrated. Bell's father decided the time was right to move to the big city of London. He had written a manuscript on visible speech and wanted to get it published. He would have a better chance of that in London than in Edinburgh.

He and Aleck moved in with Aleck's grandfather. In that house, grandfather, son, and grandson established the Headquarters and Information

Center for Visible Speech in the United Kingdom. Melly stayed in Scotland, where he took over Aleck's teaching job. In the meantime, their father took a teaching job in London.

After a year, Aleck returned to Elgin and Melly moved to London. There Melly attended college. In Elgin, Aleck Bell took a second teaching job. It was part-time at an all-girl school. He fell in love with a student there named Anna Duan. She and Bell were about the same age.

However, a teacher and student could not become romantically involved. Bell's teaching career would be ruined if such a romance were discovered. He had to be satisfied to carry Anna's picture with him. He did so for many years.[2]

Off to Bath

At the age of nineteen, Alexander Graham Bell left Elgin and took a job teaching at a college in Bath, England. It was only ninety miles from his parents' home in London. Melly returned to Scotland to teach and lecture. The youngest Bell, Ted, was scheduled to go to Elgin to take classes.

However, Ted had tuberculosis, a disease that damages the lungs and makes it hard to breathe. Today there is a vaccination to prevent tuberculosis. But that was not the case in the 1860s. Ted was so weak he spent most of his time in bed.

In spite of Ted's illness, there was some happy news in the Bell family. Melly met a woman in

Edinburgh named Carrie Ottoway and they became engaged. Although Aleck Bell was happy for his brother, he was also very jealous.[3] His headaches returned. In a letter home, Bell wrote, "In fact the only idea I can form of this past week is one immense headache."[4]

When the school year ended in Bath, Bell returned to London. He was just in time to be with his brother Ted before he died on May 17 at age eighteen. Soon afterward, Alexander Melville Bell's book, *Visible Speech: The Science of Universal Alphabetics*, was published. He dedicated the book to the memory of his son Ted.

Bell's father was pleased to have his writing in print. However, few people were interested in the book. Most felt the topic was of no use to them.

The Talking Dog

One exception was Aleck Bell. He continued to be enthusiastic about the subjects of voice and hearing and began an unusual experiment. He wondered whether mammals other than humans had the ability to speak. The Bell family had a Skye terrier. Aleck Bell tried to get the dog to make sounds as he squeezed, pinched, or pushed the dog's jaw, throat area, or mouth. In time the dog could make the sound "Ow-ah-oo-ga-mama." With some imagination, it sounded like "How are you, grandmama?"[5]

Alexander Graham Bell and his dog became local celebrities. He wrote, "The fame of the dog soon spread among my father's friends, and people came from far and near to witness the performance."[6]

A talking dog was a curiosity, but it did not bring in money. Bell took another teaching job. He taught his father's visible speech system to hearing-impaired children at the South Kensington School for the Deaf. Because it was near London, Bell did not have to move.

Bell worked with four students. In time, he taught the four to make sounds that resembled words. Meanwhile, his father began to get discouraged with the slow response to his visible speech method. In 1868 he took a trip to the United States to see whether Americans would be more interested in his idea.

While in Boston he met Gardiner Hubbard. The two men liked each other. Hubbard told Bell's father about his deaf daughter, Mabel. He explained that Mabel was born with normal hearing but had lost it when she contracted scarlet fever at age five. Hubbard appeared very interested in Bell's visible speech system. He made it known that he had raised much money for teaching deaf children. In fact, he had helped establish a school for the deaf. It was located in the western Massachusetts town of Northampton and was called the Clarke School for the Deaf.

Soon afterward, Alexander Melville Bell returned home. He raved to Aleck about America. He saw it as a land of clean air, open spaces, and opportunity.

He was so impressed that he made a major decision to move his family overseas. That would mean saying good-bye to friends and to the rest of the family. It would also mean losing business contacts and finding a new way to earn a living for both father and son. It would be a major adjustment.

The father had in mind a new home not in the United States but in Canada. Canada had a large population of Scottish immigrants. In fact, Canada's prime minister, John Macdonald, was a Scottish immigrant.

It would take some time to make the move. The Bells had to sell their house and take care of other duties before they could leave. For example, Alexander Melville Bell had already made promises to give several lectures.

There was a new member of the Bell family to make the move across the ocean. Edward Charles Ottoway Bell was born to Carrie and Melly Bell in August 1868. He would be called Ted, as Melly and Aleck's brother had been.

However, there was bad news with the good. The baby was sickly. Melly was in poor health, too. He was thin and pale and had a hacking cough. Things would get worse. In February 1870, the baby died. Just months later, Melly died from the same disease that had taken his brother's life: tuberculosis. The date was May 28, 1870. He was twenty-five years old.

At the funeral for Melly, friends and relatives noticed that Aleck Bell seemed pale and thin. Today, historians agree that he was showing symptoms of tuberculosis. However, experts differ about how deeply he was affected. Some say Bell was very sick. One book says a doctor told Bell he had only six months to live.[7] Others disagree. Brian Wood, the curator of the Bell Homestead in Brantford, Ontario, said, "Bell was in generally good shape, but he was showing early signs of tuberculosis. He was a melodramatic man who tended to exaggerate, which could be why some say he was in worse shape than he was."[8]

A Major Move

Regardless of how sick Aleck Bell truly was, his father believed he needed to move his son to a drier climate to prevent the tuberculosis from getting worse.[9] On July 21, 1870, Alexander Melville, Eliza, Alexander Graham, and Carrie Ottoway Bell boarded a ship bound for Canada.

Aleck Bell said farewell to London. He was not happy to leave behind the scholarly atmosphere of a big city with fine colleges and universities. Curator Brian Wood explained that Bell's mother helped ease his worries:

> He was afraid he was going into a backwater environment, but his mother assured him that they would be living in a social community with people he could socialize with and feel comfortable with. He was not surprised when they came here. She prepared him well.[10]

The Bell family moved into a roomy home about four miles from the center of Brantford, Ontario, Canada. It stood high on a hill overlooking the Grand River. The property included a carriage house, an ice house, a stable, and over ten acres of apple, cherry, plum, and peach trees. Bell's father named the new home Melville House.

According to Brian Wood,

> This house saved Bell's life. The climate is much drier here than in Scotland and London. If he [had] stayed in a damp climate the tuberculosis probably would have gotten much worse. Winters are colder here than in England, but much drier.[11]

Alexander Graham Bell settled into his new home with ease. He became fascinated with the Mohawk people who lived outside town. Bell met their chief, William Johnson. He told the chief he wanted to learn about the Mohawk. He said perhaps

The Bell Homestead

Bell's home is the biggest tourist attraction in Brantford, Ontario, today. Roughly eighteen thousand people visit each year. Perhaps the most famous visitor was Queen Elizabeth II in June 1997, the year of Bell's one-hundred-fiftieth birthday. During her visit, the queen unveiled a plaque designating the home a national historic site. As she toured the house and saw the old telephones inside, she marveled, "What would we ever do without the telephone?"[12]

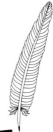

The Bells moved into this house in Brantford, Ontario, after their immigration to America in 1870.

he could teach them. At first, Chief William Johnson was unsure about this white European stranger. However, he soon accepted the fact that Bell was sincere. The Mohawk people taught Bell their war dance. In return, Bell translated the Mohawk language into visible speech.

Bell's father continued to lecture on visible speech. One of his trips took him to Boston, Massachusetts. The lecture was so successful he was invited to return. He was also offered a teaching job at the Boston School for the Deaf. However, he was fifty-two years old and not as willing to travel as before. He suggested that Aleck Bell take the teaching job. Bell accepted. In April 1871, he was on his way to Boston.

4

VOICE TO VOICE

Though Bell had been only a fair student, he was a gifted teacher. He loved the work and enjoyed the children. His pupils found him kind and patient. Any doubts the school staff had that the son could teach as well as his famous father quickly disappeared.

Bell also delivered a series of lectures that his father had been scheduled to give. At the end of one lecture, a man introduced himself to Bell. He was Gardiner Hubbard, whom Bell's father had met three years earlier. Bell remembered his father telling him about Hubbard's interest in educating the deaf. He also recalled his saying that Hubbard had a deaf daughter named Mabel.

Mabel was thirteen years old at the time. Hubbard asked Bell if he would take Mabel as a private student. Bell refused, saying he was too busy with his regular class. Instead, Mabel went to Europe to continue her education.

Within a year, Bell changed his mind about teaching a student privately. Sarah Fuller, the principal of the Boston School for the Deaf, introduced him to five-year-old George Sanders. The young boy, called Georgie by his family, had been born deaf.

Georgie was too young to attend the Boston School for the Deaf. Fuller urged Bell to take him on as a private student. She left Bell and Georgie alone. Bell found Georgie Sanders a delightful child. Despite his busy schedule, Bell decided to teach Georgie privately.

Learning with Toys

Bell noticed that two of Georgie's favorite toys were a doll and a horse. He began to play with the toys with Georgie. Sometimes he would

Alexander Graham Bell met Mabel Hubbard, seen here at the age of fourteen, for the first time in 1871, when he moved to Boston as a teacher of the deaf.

pretend to give the doll a drink of water. At other times, he would put the doll to bed or give the doll a ride on the horse. Little Georgie laughed with glee when his teacher played at his level. Bell would write the words *doll* and *horse* on a chalkboard. He would hold up the doll or horse as he wrote each word. Soon Georgie knew words and letters. In a short time he was reading and writing.

In addition to teaching, Bell began to dabble once more with inventions. One existing method of sending messages over a distance was the electric telegraph, invented by Samuel F. B. Morse in 1837. To send a telegram, a person goes to a telegraph office. There, a worker sends the person's message across a wire to a receiver by means of electric pulses. Each letter in the alphabet is represented by a different series of pulses. Quick, short sounds are called dots. Longer sounds are called dashes. For example, a series of three dots stands for the letter *S*. A dot followed by two dashes is the letter *W*. This system is called Morse code. A person at the receiving end translates the sounds into letters and words. The message is then delivered to the person meant to receive it.

Bell found it frustrating that only one telegraph message could be sent across a wire at a time. It was painfully slow. Sometimes people would stand in line for hours at a telegraph office, waiting for an open circuit to send a message. A person sending an

Samuel F. B. Morse

Although Samuel Morse is best known for developing the telegraph, inventing was not his first love. Morse hoped to earn a living as an artist. He studied art in Europe and at Yale University in Connecticut. Morse favored landscapes over portraits but found that portraits were more popular with art collectors. Although people seemed to like his art, not many bought it. In order to support his family, Morse traded his paintbrush for the telegraph.

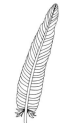

emergency message might have a long wait before it was sent. By then, it might be too late.

Bell and other inventors felt there must be a better way. Perhaps there was a method to send more than one message at a time across a wire. One person who felt the same way was a New Jersey inventor named Thomas Alva Edison. Edison and Bell worked separately to create a multiple telegraph that could send several messages at the same time.

Bell taught during the day, then worked long into the night on the multiple telegraph. As a result, he often went without sleep. He spent money on wires and tools that should have gone for food. Once again, his health began to suffer.

In the spring of 1873, Bell was offered a job as a professor of vocal physiology (the science of the voice) at Boston University. It was a good job but

Bell loved teaching and always considered himself first and foremost a teacher of the deaf. He is seen here (at top on right) in 1871 with his students at the Boston School for the Deaf.

would mean more pressure in his life. He wondered whether he should take it.

On July 1, he wrote a letter home. In it, he admitted that his poor habits were affecting his mind. He was hearing things that did not exist, and he felt he needed to see a doctor. He wrote,

> As I have scarcely had any sound sleep for many days past on account of imaginary noises at night I thought it best to consult Dr. Cotting—who recommends giving up work as soon as possible. . . . He seems to think that my mind being so much bent on the study of noises all day long may have induced these effects.[1]

He returned to his parents' home in Brantford to rest for the summer. When the temperatures began cooling down and the leaves started changing color, Bell went back to Boston. He gave up his teaching job at the Boston School for the Deaf and took the new job at Boston University.

He also continued teaching his private students, including Georgie Sanders. At the same time, he made a deal with the Sanders family. In exchange for teaching Georgie, Bell would be allowed to stay at Georgie's grandmother's house in Salem, Massachusetts, only fifteen miles from Boston. He would also be given free meals.

Everyone was happy with this arrangement. Georgie's family was pleased, since their boy was living with his grandmother. Bell's parents were happy since there would be a grandmotherly woman to watch over their son. Bell was glad because he was allowed to set up a workshop in the cellar. He was soon given the entire third floor of the house as well.

Mabel

Bell took on more private students. One of them was Mabel Hubbard. Now sixteen years old, she was growing into a beautiful young woman. She had dark hair, dark eyes, long eyelashes, and a pretty face. She was also a devoted student. During a raging snowstorm, she was Bell's only pupil to show up for her lessons.

In a short time, Bell became friendly with Mabel's family. He was often invited to the Hubbards' house for dinner. Afterward, Bell would entertain the Hubbard family by playing the piano. In addition to his other talents, Bell was a skilled piano player.

While visiting the Hubbards one day, Bell told Gardiner Hubbard about his idea of the multiple telegraph. He could not have picked a better person to tell.

Although the telegraph was the fastest way of sending messages, only one major company, Western Union, provided telegraph service. Without serious competition, Western Union could charge whatever prices it wanted and could serve its customers however it wished.

Hubbard felt Western Union was not giving Americans the chance to make full use of the telegraph. He felt that if the company had more competitors, prices would be lower, service would be better, and everyone would benefit. He thought Bell's idea was superb. If the multiple telegraph could work, then perhaps a new company could be started. Western Union would then have the competition Hubbard felt it needed.

Hubbard offered to help Bell in his attempt to develop the multiple telegraph. He gave him money to buy parts. He also helped him in legal matters.

For one thing, Bell would have to apply for a patent from the federal government.

A patent is a document that states the name of the inventor of any device. With a patent, Bell would have proof that he was the inventor. If he did not have a patent, then anybody could claim that he or she was the inventor. The patent would protect Bell's exclusive right to make, sell, and use his invention.

Bell told Hubbard that he had also discussed the multiple telegraph with Georgie Sanders's father, Thomas. Sanders was also interested in the idea. Sanders was a wealthy man, and contributed money to Bell's experiments. Because both Hubbard and Sanders gave Bell money to help complete his invention, Bell planned to share any profits made from the multiple telegraph with both men.

But the multiple telegraph was not Bell's only idea. He was also working on something called an autograph telegraph. It would transmit a message in a person's actual handwriting. There was also the "telephone." It would carry the human voice across a wire.

Hubbard and Sanders liked the multiple telegraph, but thought little of Bell's other ideas. Tom Hutchinson, telephone historian for Bell Atlantic in Boston, said, "They saw no future as backers of the telephone. They thought it was a toy. Even if it was perfected to working condition, they thought it would have no practical use. They wanted him to spend his time on the multiple telegraph."[2]

Meanwhile, Thomas Edison was having success making a multiple telegraph in his New Jersey lab. First, he developed a duplex telegraph system, which allowed two messages to travel over one wire at the same time in opposite directions. Shortly afterward, he invented a quadruplex telegraph system. This new system permitted four messages to be sent at the same time. To Hubbard and Sanders, Edison's success made no difference. Edison was doing his research for Hubbard's hated Western Union.

Thomas Watson

Bell was intelligent and creative, but he was not skill-ful with his hands. He needed an assistant, someone who could help build his inventions.

One day in early 1874, Bell entered a Boston machine shop owned by a man named Charles Williams. What better place to find a quality mechanic? Bell asked Williams to recommend some-one who could help him. Williams suggested a nineteen-year-old man named Thomas Watson.

Watson was sitting at a bench, working on a pro-ject for an inventor named Moses Farmer. Watson later remembered,

> One day early in 1874 when I was hard at work for Mr. Farmer on his apparatus for exploding submarine mines by electricity and wondering what was coming next, there came rushing out of the office door and through the shop to my workbench a tall, slender,

quick-motioned young man with a pale face, black side-whiskers and drooping mustache, big nose and high, sloping forehead crowned with bushy jet-black hair. It was Alexander Graham Bell, a young professor in Boston University, whom I then saw for the first time.[3]

Bell and Watson struck up a partnership and worked on the multiple telegraph. They made little progress, though. Bell began to lose interest in the project and became more and more excited about the idea of transmitting the human voice over a wire.

The Phonautograph

Shortly after Bell met Watson, Bell gave a lecture at the nearby Massachusetts Institute of Technology (MIT), one of the most respected technical colleges in the world.

While at MIT, Bell was given a chance to tour the institute's laboratories. In one lab was a machine called a phonautograph. It had been invented in France in 1851 by a man named Leon Scott. The phonautograph had a mouthpiece, a membrane that was similar

Nineteen-year-old Thomas Watson became Bell's partner in 1874.

Unusual Partners

Bell and Watson could not have been more different from each other. Bell was educated and well read. He knew how to charm people by saying the right words at the right time. Although Watson was intelligent, he was uneducated and lacked proper manners. The only utensil he used to eat food was a knife. Watson later wrote, "I was much embarrassed the first time I had supper with Bell at his boarding house, in trying to imitate his exclusive use of a fork in the conveyance of food."[4] Yet in spite of their differences, the two men worked well together.

to a human eardrum, a wooden lever, and a bristle. When a person spoke into the mouthpiece, the voice vibrations against the membrane caused the lever and bristle to move. The bristle then drew lines of the vibrations across a pane of smoked glass. In other words, the phonautograph made a picture of the human voice. Bell thought the phonautograph was fascinating.

Since Bell had done so much work teaching deaf people, he was familiar with the workings of the human ear. He knew that when people speak, their voices create waves in the air. When these waves reach the eardrum, they make a sound. In a way, the phonautograph did the same thing.

But the phonautograph only made a picture of the human voice. What about the voice itself?

Bell returned to Brantford in the summer of 1874. He spent a great deal of time that summer thinking about what he had learned. Bell Homestead curator Brian Wood said,

> Bell had a favorite spot he went to near his parents' home, which he called his dreaming place, on a hill overlooking the Grand River. He did some of his best thinking there, and it was there one day that summer that he came up with the concept of the telephone.[5]

Bell all but gave up on the idea of the multiple telegraph. When he returned to Boston that fall, the telephone was the only invention on which he spent any time. Thomas Watson later noted,

> Although Bell did not realize it at the time, it was lucky for him his telegraph apparatus did not work any better, for had it been an easy success the coming of the telephone might have been delayed and, perhaps, have found its way into the world through some other brain.[6]

In fact, there was no real reason for Bell to spend any more time on the multiple telegraph. Telephone historian Tom Hutchinson said, "If the telephone could work, it would make the multiple telegraph unnecessary."[7]

By then, Bell had spent a great deal of Hubbard's and Sanders's money. He was hesitant to ask them for any more. Bell's father had a wealthy friend named George Brown. Bell asked Brown if he would help finance the telephone idea. Brown agreed.

Brown said he would apply for a patent in Great Britain for the telephone. That meant that Bell could not apply for a patent in the United States. If he did, the British patent would not be legal.

Brown planned to sail to England to file the patent in person. Bell did not say anything about this to Hubbard or Sanders.

Teaching Again

Bell could not spend all his time inventing. He had to earn money. He was not getting paid to tinker with a possible invention. So he continued teaching both his private students and his Boston University students. Since he loved teaching, it was not a great hardship.

In addition, something else was taking up his time. Bell was spending many hours at the Hubbard home. It was not only to fulfill his duties as a teacher. Bell had fallen in love with Mabel Hubbard. He thought she was pretty, and he also found her very intelligent. He enjoyed talking with her.

At first Mabel's parents were uneasy about Bell dating their daughter. He was ten years older than she, and they believed she was too young for him. Mabel felt the same at first, but Bell did not give up. He took the time to convince both Mabel and her parents how much in love he was. In time, Mabel began to realize that she, too, was in love. Her parents realized it, too. At that time, it was proper for a man to ask a woman's father for permission to marry his daughter. Bell did so, and Gardiner Hubbard approved.

Bell began to spend even more time at the Hubbard home. It turned out to be a good experience for him. Until this time Gardiner Hubbard had insisted that Bell work on a multiple telegraph instead of the "silly" telephone idea. But because of Bell's many visits, historian Tom Hutchinson explained,

> Gardiner Hubbard heard Bell talk so much about the telephone and saw how excited he was about it. He also saw how much his daughter liked him. So he gave him some slack on the multiple telegraph.
>
> He [Hubbard] wouldn't let Bell give up totally on the telegraph. He had him put it on the back burner.[8]

The Laboratory on the Fourth Floor

During the last days of 1875, Bell moved from the Sanders home into his own apartment at 5 Exeter Place in the center of Boston. Today, the area is occupied by tall office buildings. In Bell's day, it was filled with private homes and clip-clopping carriages on cobblestone streets. Bell and Watson set up a laboratory on the fourth floor of the building. There, they worked long into the night and early morning. Watson spent so much time there that he finally moved in with Bell.

In early 1876, Bell and Watson perfected a design for their telephone. The next step was to go to Washington, D.C., and apply for a patent. Bell had no choice but to tell Gardiner Hubbard about his business deal with George Brown. He told Hubbard

Gardiner and Gertrude Hubbard, Mabel's parents, came to know
Bell, and gave their permission for the two to marry.

that he must wait to apply for a patent until he heard
from Brown. What he did not realize was that Brown
had given up on Bell's telephone. The more Brown
had thought about the idea of the human voice
being carried over a wire, the crazier it seemed.[9]

Hubbard and Bell kept waiting to hear from
Brown about a British patent. Finally, Hubbard ran
out of patience. He went to Washington, D.C., on
his own on February 14, 1876. There, he applied for
a patent for the telephone in Bell's name.

It was lucky for Bell that his future father-in-law had filed his patent application. About an hour later, an inventor named Elisha Gray applied for a caveat for the telephone. Caveats are no longer used, but at that time a person could file a caveat for a preliminary idea of an invention. It meant that he or she was working on a specific invention but had not completed it yet. When the invention was perfected, that person would then apply for a patent.

Birth of the Telephone

On the night of March 10, 1876, Bell and Watson were working in separate rooms about fifteen feet apart. In Bell's room was a transmitter. In Watson's was a receiver. A wire connected these two parts of their test telephone. Watson stood by a dresser with his ear to the receiver. Suddenly he heard a crackling sound. Then he heard Bell's voice. It was the first telephone message in history.

What were the first words spoken over the telephone? Watson wrote in his autobiography that Bell had accidentally spilled battery acid on himself and called Watson for help. Watson wrote that Bell's words were, "Mr. Watson, come here, I want you!"[10]

That version of the story has long been accepted as the truth, and those words have become famous. However, historian Tom Hutchinson disagrees, saying: "Those are the words written down for posterity. But if you had spilled battery acid on

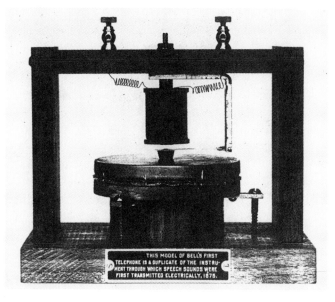

This is a model of the first telephone through which the human voice was successfully transmitted.

yourself, you would probably not say something so calmly. You'd probably be swearing."[11]

The truth will likely never be known. The important thing is that the telephone worked.

It was later that year, in June 1876, that Bell demonstrated his telephone to Dom Pedro and other dignitaries at the Centennial Exhibition.

In August, Bell's father made a telephone call from his home in Brantford. Bell received the call at a store in the town of Paris, Ontario. The two towns were eight miles apart. This was the first long-distance call ever.

5

A BABY NAMED PHOTOPHONE?

In 1876, Alexander Graham Bell was a happy man. He had no reason not to be. He was engaged to the woman he loved. The invention into which he had put so much work was successful.

Within a year, long-distance telephone conversations between Bell and Watson were covering greater distances than that between Paris and Brantford, Ontario. Some were made between Boston and Salem, Massachusetts, fifteen miles apart. Others were between Boston, Massachusetts, and Providence, Rhode Island, a distance of fifty miles. Yet another connected phones in Boston and New York City, over two hundred miles apart.

Snyder County Library
Selinsgrove PA

The purpose of these long-distance calls was not simply for testing. They were a way for Bell and Watson to advertise their new invention. In Bell's day, most people advertised their products or services in newspapers. But would people buy something they had never seen work? To solve that problem, Bell advertised in newspapers that he would demonstrate his invention in certain places. A typical ad said:

> *Every man, woman and child should carefully examine the workings of Prof. Bell's speaking and singing telephone.*[1]

In a short time, thousands of curious people were showing up to see this new marvel.

Bell was a handsome figure. With his tall, slim frame and dark hair and beard, he drew people's attention. For a typical demonstration, Bell would

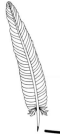

Celebrating Success
One time in 1876 Bell and Watson tested an early long-distance call between the neighboring cities of Boston and Cambridge, Massachusetts. After this successful test, they returned to their apartment and celebrated loudly. They were so loud that their landlady scolded them. She told them not to make so much noise again or she would kick them out of the building. They made an effort to be more quiet after that.

travel to a city while Watson stayed in Boston. Bell would set up his equipment in an auditorium and connect his telephone to telegraph wires. He would then call Watson and begin a conversation with him. Watson would respond by saying, "Good evening," "How do you do?" or "What do you think of the telephone?"[2] He would often sing a song through the telephone for the audience. He was not a very good singer.[3] However, he said, "My singing was always a hit. The telephone obscured its defects and gave it a mystic touch."[4]

First Telephone Poem

In May 1877, Bell and Watson did a demonstration in Lawrence, Massachusetts. The next morning *The Lawrence American* published the first poem about the telephone. It was written from the point of view of a person in the audience waiting for the demonstration to begin. The poem was called "Waiting for Watson." Part of it went this way:

> *To the great hall we strayed,*
> *Fairly our fee was paid,*
> *Seven hundred there delayed,*
> *But, where was Watson?*
> *Oh, how our ears we strained,*
> *How our hopes waxed and waned,*
> *Patience to dregs we drained,*
> *Yes, we did, Watson!*
> *Give but one lusty groan,*
> *For bread we'll take a stone,*
> *Ring your old telephone!*
> *Ring, brother Watson!*[5]

Watson remembered how he and Bell had disturbed their landlady by making too much noise. He did not want that to happen again. So he came up with a clever idea. He made a soundproof tunnel with some barrel staffs and blankets from his and Bell's beds. It became the first telephone booth.

Soon the first telephone company was formed. Bell, Watson, Gardiner Hubbard, and Thomas Sanders were the founding members of the Bell Telephone Company. They soon started a second business called New England Telephone Company. It made money by licensing people to use Bell's telephone patent.

Marriage

On July 11, 1877, Alexander Graham Bell and Mabel Hubbard were married at the Hubbard home in Cambridge, Massachusetts. The Bells took a long honeymoon. First, they went to Niagara Falls, then to Brantford so that Mabel could meet Bell's family. While they were visiting, Bell's mother broke an oat cake over Mabel's head. It was an old Scottish custom that was supposed to bring good fortune to the newlyweds.

Alexander and Mabel Bell then boarded a steamship that took them across the Atlantic Ocean. They spent the rest of their honeymoon in England and Scotland. However, it turned into a business trip. Bell spent the next year and a half traveling through England demonstrating the telephone.

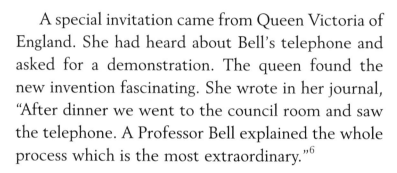

A Special Gift
One of the first things Bell did with the money he earned from the telephone was to give Mabel an expensive gift, even though he still needed money for himself. It was a silver model of a telephone.

A special invitation came from Queen Victoria of England. She had heard about Bell's telephone and asked for a demonstration. The queen found the new invention fascinating. She wrote in her journal, "After dinner we went to the council room and saw the telephone. A Professor Bell explained the whole process which is the most extraordinary."[6]

No to Darwina, Yes to Elsie May

In England, Mabel Bell gave birth to the couple's first child on May 8, 1878. At first, Bell wanted to name his daughter Darwina in honor of Charles Darwin. Bell was a great admirer of Darwin, the British naturalist who first made popular the theory of evolution.

Mabel, however, would have nothing to do with such an unusual name for her child. The baby was named Elsie May. Elsie was a form of Bell's mother's name, Eliza. May was a nickname for Mabel. It was also the month of the baby's birth.

Soon after Elsie was born, Bell sneaked into her room and, without warning, blew a trumpet.

According to Bell, "Mabel never moved, but the little one flung out its arms and legs and shrieked in terror."[7] Bell saw for himself that Elsie May's hearing was just fine.

At first, Bell's success seemed to agree with him. He gained needed weight, and his headaches mostly disappeared. That did not last long.

While still overseas, Bell received word that Western Union was starting its own telephone company. It was called the American Speaking Telephone Company. Among the company's owners was Elisha Gray, the inventor who had filed for a caveat just an hour after Bell had applied for a patent for his telephone. Working for Western Union with Gray was Thomas Edison.

Western Union claimed that Gray, not Bell, was the original inventor of the telephone. They avoided conflict with Bell's patent by giving their telephone a different design.

Bell was disgusted and became physically ill over the matter. His headaches returned.[8] Although he was a determined inventor, Bell did not have the will to fight a huge company like Western Union. He wrote a letter to Thomas Watson, saying he would give up the telephone business and move to Quebec to teach. He did not have the stomach to deal with the world of business.

Watson had a large stake in Bell's decision. If Bell gave up his rights to the telephone, Watson and all the other investors would lose any future earnings from the invention.

The Bells docked in Quebec in November 1878. There to meet them was Watson. Thomas Watson later wrote that when he arrived at the dock, he

> found Bell even more dissatisfied with the telephone business than his letters had indicated. He told me he wasn't going to have anything more to do with it, but was going to take up teaching again as soon as he could get a position. I gave him as clear a picture as I could of what we had accomplished in the United States, painting the future of the telephone business there in bright colors.[9]

Finally, Watson wore Bell down. Bell said he would go to Boston to fight the matter after visiting his father in Brantford. Watson went to Brantford with Bell. He wanted to make sure Bell would not change his mind. After several days, Bell took a train to Boston to begin preparing evidence to fight Western Union in court.

While the legal battles were being fought, Bell and his partners merged their two businesses. Bell Telephone Company and New England Telephone Company formed the National Bell Telephone Company on March 13, 1879. It reached across the country.

Bell's patent battle lasted for a year. It was the most complicated legal case concerning a patent in United States history up to that time.[10] Bell was called to testify time and time again. He had to show notes and letters that he had written years earlier while working on the telephone. To find those papers, he and Watson searched every corner and file of their lab.

After much looking, they found one paper that clinched the case. It was a letter Elisha Gray himself had written to Bell. In the letter, Gray credited Bell as the sole inventor of the telephone.

Gray and his lawyers knew their case was doomed. Gray said to his lawyers about the letter, "I'll swear to it and you can swear at it."[11]

After the case was decided in Bell's favor, his telephone company was given new life. People began investing their money in it. The value of its stock soared. Bell would never have money problems again.

The telephone was catching on. In 1879, Rutherford B. Hayes became the first president to have a telephone in the White House. Bell gave up on the idea of moving to Quebec. He did not return to Boston, either. Mabel's family had moved to Washington, D.C., so in 1879 the Bells rented a home in Washington to be near them. Watson decided to stay in Boston, and the two friends parted ways. Bell found a new assistant named Charles Sumner Tainter.

A New Invention and a New Arrival

The team of Bell and Tainter worked together as smoothly as Bell and Watson had. Early in 1880 they

The Bell family sat for this portrait in 1885. Left to right are Elsie, Mabel, Marian, and Alexander Graham Bell.

began working on a new kind of telephone. It would be wireless. Bell called it a photophone. With the photophone, the human voice would be carried by a beam of light instead of over a wire. On February 15, 1880, Bell and Tainter tested it outdoors. It worked!

Later that day Mabel gave birth to another girl. Bell was so happy with his new invention that he considered naming the baby Photophone. Again, Mabel would not give her child a strange name. The baby was named Marian but nicknamed Daisy.

In the meantime, some people still claimed Bell had stolen the idea of the telephone. Bell was called into court to testify over and over. He continued to win each case.

The government of France had no trouble believing Bell. They awarded him the Volta Prize, a respected scientific honor. With the Volta Prize, Bell was awarded fifty thousand French francs, equal to ten thousand United States dollars at the time.[12] Bell used the money to found the Volta Laboratory in Washington, D.C., for scientific experiments.

6

NEW INVENTIONS, NEW FRIENDS, NEW SCOTLAND

Some inventors do their best work early in the morning. Alexander Graham Bell was not one of them. He loved working at night. Much of the time he would stay up until four o'clock in the morning perfecting his inventions. He said, "To take night from me is to rob me of life."[1]

Though Bell enjoyed teaching, the money he earned from the telephone allowed him to quit his daytime job. He could then work the hours during which he was most productive. Telephone historian Tom Hutchinson said, "He found he liked experimentation even better than teaching."[2]

Staying up late forced Bell to sleep in the next morning. Often he would not wake up until eleven o'clock. Mabel could not stand her husband's hours. She wrote in her diary, "Our worst quarrels have always been about that."[3]

Overall, the Bells had a happy marriage. Yet there were times that tested its strength. The second half of 1881 proved to be one of those times.

Strange Fate

Who knew that the paths of one of the world's premier inventors, the president of the United States, and a crazed assassin would soon cross?

On July 2, a lone gunman named Charles Guiteau shot United States President James A. Garfield at a Washington train station. One bullet entered the president's arm. The other went into his back near the spine. Garfield was severely injured. However, it seemed he would not die, and he returned to the White House.

The bullet in Garfield's arm was not of major concern. The bullet in his back was. Nobody knew exactly in what part of Garfield's back the bullet was stuck. Today an X-ray machine can be used for this type of case. But there were no X-ray machines in 1881. Doctors tried to find the bullet by probing the wound with their fingers. At the time it was not known how important cleanliness was when dealing with sick people. Doctors attending Garfield poked dirty hands into his wound.

By then Bell was well known for his work with electricity. Garfield's staff asked Bell to try to invent something that would locate the bullet in a safer and less painful way. Bell and Tainter did their best in a very short time. On the evening of July 26, the two men entered the White House with a makeshift bullet probe made of batteries, coils, and wires. Bell and Tainter hoped it would vibrate when it located the bullet.

The bullet probe did not work that evening. The men discovered they had incorrectly connected a part of the machine called the condenser. They tried again on August 1. At first, the machine appeared to work. It vibrated over a large area of the president's wounded body. But then, the men realized the vibration was over too large an area to be caused by a bullet. Something was wrong.

Bell asked one of Garfield's doctors what the bed was made of. The doctor answered that the bed was wood but the bedsprings were steel. No wonder the bullet probe registered over such a large area. The steel bedsprings were interfering with the bullet probe's signal.

The doctors told Bell that Garfield was too weak to be moved onto a wooden bed. The experiment was useless.

Some Americans said that Bell's experiments had made Garfield sicker and weaker. Others claimed that Bell took advantage of the president's weak condition to earn glory and money for himself. Bell was troubled by such talk.

One of Bell's inventions—the bullet probe—was used to try to save the life of President James A. Garfield, seen here, after an assassination attempt in July 1881.

That summer a man named John Michels got in touch with Bell. Michels was editor of a weekly magazine called *Science*. He wanted Bell to buy the company that published *Science*. He needed somebody with money to help keep his magazine in business. An inventor such as Bell seemed a likely choice to be owner of a magazine devoted to scientific news. But Bell was too busy trying to save the president's life.

The Bells had even more on their minds that summer. On August 15, Mabel gave birth to a boy two months prematurely. He was named Edward, in memory of Bell's younger brother. The baby died a few hours later from respiratory failure.

To help get over his sorrow, Bell threw himself more deeply into his work. He kept trying to perfect his bullet probe. He experimented with it by placing a bullet in raw beef and scanning his machine over the meat. Bell and Tainter decided

Garfield was too weak for any more tests. They were right. The president died on September 19.

Doctors performed an autopsy on Garfield's body. They discovered that the bullet had not caused Garfield's death. He had died from infection caused by the constant probing of his wound. The autopsy also showed that the bullet was too deep inside Garfield's body for Bell's machine to detect it.

These sad events took a toll on the Bells' well-being. In spite of all their wealth and fame, in the fall of 1881, they were not happy. In response, they did something most people without their money could not do. They decided to get away from all their problems by sailing to Europe for a long trip.

Although they could run away from home, they could not escape their memories. The thoughts of

The President's Assassin

Garfield's assassin, Charles Guiteau, was charged with first-degree murder of the president. His lawyer did not deny that Guiteau shot and killed Garfield. However, he tried an unusual defense for the time. He claimed that Guiteau was insane and could not stop himself from committing the crime. The jurors at the trial did not accept the defense, and Guiteau was found guilty of murder. He was hanged for his crime in 1882.

baby Edward gasping for air stayed inside Bell's mind. He began designing a mechanical device to help people breathe.

Bell called it a vacuum jacket. It was an iron cylinder that covered a person's body up to his or her neck. Air pressure would be forced in and out of the jacket with a hand bellows. Bell worked on it while on vacation in Europe. In England he demonstrated it for a group of doctors. However, most experts did not think it would be of use except to help drowning victims.

Failed *Science*

The Bells returned home in the spring of 1882. They were ready to return to the real world. They bought a home in Washington, D.C. The house and grounds together covered a city block. That summer John Michels again approached Bell about buying *Science* magazine. Unlike the previous year, Bell's mind was clear of distractions. He agreed to enter the magazine business.

One problem with the magazine was that not enough people were willing to buy copies of it each week. The magazine needed six thousand subscribers to break even financially.[4] It did not come close. Bell lost money on this business decision. However, *Science* would not be the last magazine in which Bell would take an interest.

November 10, 1882, was a special date in Bell's life. That day he officially became a United States citizen. It seemed as if it would be a happy time for the Bell household. Mabel was pregnant once again. On November 17, Bell was at a meeting of the National Academy of Sciences in Hartford, Connecticut. He had no idea that back in Washington, Mabel had gone into premature labor. A boy she named Robert was born. He died within a matter of hours. Bell returned home three hours later to learn that his son had been born and died that day. The Bells would have no more children.

As usual, Bell coped with his grief by diving headfirst into his many projects. However, there was one that he wanted less and less to do with. That was the telephone.

The telephone was not doing poorly. On the contrary, it had changed the daily lives of thousands of Americans. Usually the first people in a town to sign up for telephone service were doctors and pharmacists. Drugstores provided a special service to their customers by letting them use their telephones for free. Soon these customers wanted telephones in their own homes, and sales soared. In 1881, just five years after Bell patented the telephone, there were almost seventy thousand telephones in the United States.[5] By 1882, the total was ninety thousand.[6] In 1883, it was over one hundred twenty-three thousand.[7]

Not everyone was thrilled with the new invention. Mark Twain, the most successful author of his day, thought it was an invasion of privacy. One December, Twain offered the following Christmas season wish:

> It is my heart-warm and world-embracing Christmas hope and aspiration that all of us, the high, the low, the rich, the poor, the admired, the despised, the loved, the hated, the civilized, the savage (every man and brother of us all throughout the whole earth), may eventually be gathered together in a heaven of everlasting rest and peace and bliss, except the inventor of the telephone.[8]

Twain was the exception, though. Most people welcomed the telephone. They used it to conduct business.

Dishonest people realized how much money Bell was making. Again and again Bell had to face lawsuits from people who claimed that they and not

Telephone Operators

In the early days of the telephone, one could not directly dial another person's home. Telephone operators were hired to connect telephone calls on a panel of electrical circuits called a switchboard. Boys as young as twelve were hired to be operators. That turned out to be a huge mistake. Most of the boys were not mature enough to deal with the public. They became known for their rudeness to customers. When not insulting people, they threw spitballs and flung rubber bands at each other. The boys were eventually replaced by young women, who dealt with customers in a more civil manner.

Bell had invented the telephone. Some had never even handled a telephone. Throughout the 1880s, Bell successfully defended his patent in more than six hundred lawsuits.[9]

Good-bye, Telephone Company

Finally Bell gave up. He was tired of all the hassles. Gilbert Grosvenor, a descendant of Bell, said, "Once the telephone worked—once he proved his point—he lost interest in it. It was a done thing. He just wanted to get on to other things."[10]

By the early 1880s, Bell no longer played an active part in the day-to-day operations of any telephone business. However, he remained an owner and stockholder of the company he created and continued to receive profits from it.

A new field Bell was ready to tackle was recorded sound. Thomas Edison had patented the phonograph in 1877. He recorded "Mary Had a Little Lamb" on a cylinder covered with tinfoil. Bell thought he could do better.

Much of the money to fund Bell's newest inventions came from the Volta Laboratory. Bell's most promising creation was a flat disk with a wax coating. A stylus was used to etch sounds onto the wax. A needle was used to play back the sounds. It would in time be called a phonograph record.

Bell and Edison were not the only famous inventors to develop new products in the late 1800s. It was a time of extraordinary innovation, with thousands, and even hundreds of thousands, of patents being issued each year. George Eastman had invented a process for making dry photographic plates. This led to the first easy-to-use camera. George Selden crafted a three-cylinder internal combustion engine, which he used to power one of the first automobiles. William Burroughs patented the adding machine, and George Westinghouse built the first successful alternating current power plant in the United States.

However, Bell and Edison were the two most famous inventors of their time. Although they competed, historians say they were never bitter toward each other. Telephone historian Tom Hutchinson called them "friendly rivals."[11] Douglas Tarr, a reference archivist at Edison National Historic Site in West Orange, New Jersey, said, "Although they never worked together, Edison did not consider Bell a rival. There was no great hostility between them."[12]

The Bells suffered another tragedy in the summer of 1885. Mabel's sister fell ill and died. Once again the Bells took a trip to escape their grief. They went to the Canadian territory of Newfoundland and the province of Nova Scotia in extreme eastern Canada.

At the easternmost end of Nova Scotia is remote Cape Breton Island. Bell fell in love with the land. The rough hills and the swooping glens reminded him of his native Scotland. The Bells decided to build a second home near a town called Baddeck. They chose a spot on a hill called Red Head Mountain. It overlooked two channels of Bras d'Or Lake. This new home would be a retreat from the muggy summers of Washington, D.C.

Aynsley MacFarlane, the site manager of Alexander Graham Bell National Historic Site in Baddeck, said,

> There were three different things that drew Bell here: the scenery, the climate, and the people. The bulk of the new settlers here had come from Scotland. In fact, the name Nova Scotia means New Scotland in Latin. As someone of Scottish descent, he felt right at home.[13]

A Special Six-Year-Old

Well known for his inventions and work with the deaf, Bell was sought out by people needing help or favors. One day in early 1887, Bell had a most interesting visitor at his house in Washington. She was a six-year-old girl named Helen Keller. With her was her father, Captain Arthur H. Keller. They had come to Washington from the small town of Tuscumbia, Alabama.

When Helen was nineteen months old, she became ill with a high fever. The family doctors said she had "acute congestion of the stomach and brain."[14] That was a very general term. It has never been determined exactly what illness she had, but it left her unable to hear or see.[15] Her father thought it might have damaged her brain.

Bell picked up little Helen and placed her on his knee. He gave her his watch to hold. She turned it over and held it against her body. Bell could tell she was reacting to the vibrations it made. That convinced him that she had no brain damage.

Helen Keller later wrote, "He understood my signs, and I knew and loved him at once. But I did not dream that that interview would be the door through which I should pass from darkness into light, from isolation into friendship, companionship, knowledge, love."[16]

Bell recommended that Helen's father contact a man named Michael Anagnos. Anagnos was the director of a school for the blind in Boston called the Perkins Institution. Anagnos recommended that Helen work with a special teacher named Anne Mansfield Sullivan, known to her friends as Annie.

Within a year, Sullivan had done an amazing job communicating with Helen. The small girl was breaking out of her world of silence and darkness. Sullivan got Helen to understand that things had names. By the middle of 1888, Helen was reading and writing letters, using a special alphabet for the blind called Braille.

Also in 1888, Mabel Bell's father, Gardiner Hubbard, founded a group in Washington called the National Geographic Society. Its purpose was to celebrate exploration and discovery. The society also published a journal called *National Geographic Magazine*. Bell had little to do with his father-in-law's project. He was too busy working on his inventions and helping people such as Helen Keller.

In time Keller wrote more and more letters to Bell. He sent one letter she wrote him to a newspaper in New York to be published. Thanks in part to Bell, Keller and Sullivan were becoming famous. Within a couple of years Bell wrote, "The public have already become interested in Helen Keller, and through her, may perhaps be led to take an interest in the more general subject of the Education of the Deaf."[17]

Bell certainly did his part. In 1890 he founded an organization called the American Association for the Promotion of the Teaching of Speech to the Deaf (AAPTSD). It was formed to promote visible speech, Bell's favorite way of teaching the deaf.

Alexander Graham Bell helped introduce Helen Keller (left) to teacher Anne Sullivan (center). Keller would go on to become a famous writer and speaker, despite being both blind and deaf. She would also remain a close friend of Bell's.

Around the same time a man named Edward Gallaudet was promoting a different way of teaching the deaf. It was called sign language. In sign language, deaf people communicate by making hand gestures instead of sounds. Bell disliked the idea of sign language. He thought it made the hearing-impaired stand out. Bell and Gallaudet disagreed to the point of expressing open anger at each other. Still, Bell allowed those supporting sign language to hold important posts in his AAPTSD. Anyone interested in helping the hearing-impaired was welcome.

Soon Alexander Graham Bell would be welcoming friends such as Helen Keller to the family's new home in Nova Scotia.

7

INTO THE AIR

The Bells moved into a lodge on Red Head Mountain in Baddeck, Nova Scotia, in 1890. The lodge was a part-time second home until their permanent one was completed. Bell decided to call his home Beinn Bhreagh. *Beinn Bhreagh* is Gaelic for "beautiful mountain." It is pronounced *ben vreeah*.

By the time Bell settled into the lodge, he was in his early forties. He was no longer the dark-haired man with the sturdy build of his younger days. His hair had turned gray, and he had gained weight around the middle. But his habits had not changed. He still liked to stay up late at night to work. Mabel was still frustrated by his hours.

The Bells' house in Nova Scotia was known as Beinn Bhreagh, which means "beautiful mountain."

The open spaces in the countryside of Baddeck gave Bell the chance to raise sheep. He could not have done so while living in cities such as Boston or Washington. Since a sheep is close to the size of a human being, Bell thought the animal would be a good test subject for his vacuum jacket. Bell had been working on the vacuum jacket off and on since his son Edward had died in 1881.

One day, one of Bell's sheep was found nearly drowned. It was unconscious and did not move. With Bell's vacuum jacket, the sheep was revived.

One of the men working on the construction of Bell's house was shocked by what seemed to be a sheep coming back to life from the dead. He quit working for Bell on the spot.

The Bells made themselves at home in Nova Scotia. They met new people and enjoyed entertaining. However, they were disappointed by one thing they noticed about their neighbors. Those of different religions and political beliefs rarely mixed. Mabel decided to form a social club that would allow all people to join. Nobody would be kept out because of religious or political views.

She called her group the Young Ladies Club of Baddeck. It was typical to have separate clubs for men and for women. In 1891 Mabel's club had its first meeting. It went very well, and many more meetings followed.

Mabel described one club meeting in a letter to her daughter Elsie. She wrote,

> Yesterday was lovely. The Ladies Club Board came over for a meeting at four o'clock. We talked until five-thirty and then got out our needlework or knitting and gossiped until six, had a jolly dinner and then Papa [Bell] showed us lantern slides until (eight-thirty when) our guests departed and we felt we had a beautiful long evening. I tell you what, there is nothing like real country life when you know how to manage it so that you have real sociability. I have more of this here than I do in Washington.[1]

Sometimes Mabel would go to Baddeck by herself while Bell stayed in Washington. Other times she might be in Europe with Elsie and Daisy while Bell was in Baddeck. Still, Aynsley MacFarlane said, "They might not have always traveled together every time, but this was their family home and they were usually together here as a family. It wasn't just during the summer, either. They were here through some winters."[2]

Mabel Bell's life in Baddeck was more than one big party. She also acted as her husband's business advisor. For example, she would tell him when it was the right time to apply for a patent.

Into the Sky

When not busy with his vacuum jacket, Bell worked on an invention that would take him to new heights: a flying machine.

Like the telephone in the 1870s, many people in the 1890s were working on flying machines. The airplanes that we take for granted today did not yet exist. But forward-thinking people in the 1890s thought they could. They felt that if birds could fly,

A Social Family

The Bells loved to socialize. Every summer in Baddeck they held a big party they called the Harvest Home Celebration. Many of their Washington, D.C., friends came. There were Scottish games, Scottish dancing, and much food. Despite their hard work, the Bells enjoyed a busy social schedule.

why couldn't people invent a machine that would use the same principles?

Among those who were trying to invent a flying machine was Samuel Langley. Langley was a well-respected astronomer. He was also secretary of the Smithsonian Institution, the famous museum and research complex in Washington, D.C. Langley was twelve years older than Bell, and, like Bell, he had been a college professor. He had not attended college but had learned on his own by reading books.

In 1891 Langley was in Washington, where he was scheduled to give a series of lectures about the idea that people might someday be able to fly. At the time, Bell was in Baddeck and Mabel was at the family's Washington home. Mabel read about Langley's talks in local newspapers and wrote to her husband about them. Soon Bell was back in Washington to meet Samuel Langley. Because of their common interest in flight experimentation, the two men became good friends.

Sometimes Bell visited Langley at his home in Virginia, just outside Washington, D.C. At other times, Langley visited Bell in Baddeck. By 1893 the Bells had plenty of room to host guests such as Langley. Their mansion in Baddeck, Beinn Bhreagh, was completed. A newspaper at the time described it as "the finest mansion in eastern Canada."[3]

In 1893 there was another world's fair. This one was in Chicago. Bell took a special guest with him to visit it. She was Helen Keller, now twelve years old. Joining them was Helen's teacher, Annie Sullivan.

Although she was deaf and blind, Helen Keller was well known for writing short stories and poems. At the fair, she drew a great deal of attention from other visitors. She later wrote,

> Dr. Bell went everywhere with us and in his own delightful way described to me the objects of greatest interest. In the electrical building we examined the telephones, autophones, phonographs, and other inventions, and he made me understand how it is possible to send a message on wires that mock space and outrun time.[4]

Like most girls her age, Helen liked taking a break from things such as science. At one point a woman named Carolyn Talcott was in charge of protecting Helen. Helen asked, "Miss Talcott, is anybody watching us?" When Talcott answered no, Helen cheerfully responded, "Then let's romp."[5] In Helen's day, that was a way of saying, "Let's have some fun."

Back in Baddeck and Washington, Bell had his fun devoting time to his flying experiments. In 1893 he said to a reporter, "I have not the shadow of a doubt that the problem of aerial navigation will be solved within 10 years."[6]

Kites, Rotors, and Propellers

Bell spent his days flying kites and testing rotors and propellers like those on helicopters today. Then in

May 1896, Bell visited Langley's houseboat in Quantico, Virginia. Langley was about to test a sixteen-foot-long, steam-powered, propeller-driven airplane model he had created.

Langley wanted Bell as his only witness. He was concerned that a crowd of onlookers would mock him if his airplane model failed. Langley knew Bell well enough to know that he would not laugh even if the model was a flop.

There was no reason for Langley to be concerned. The plane was tested twice and flew beautifully both times.

Although flight-testing was Bell's main passion, it did not occupy all his time. He continued to remain active in groups working with the deaf. He never tired of the company of hearing-impaired children. Helen Keller wrote of Bell, "He is never quite so happy as when he has a little deaf child in his arms."[7]

He also decided to enter the world of magazine publishing once

Bell devoted a great deal of his time to experimenting with flying machines. He is seen here at center, testing a kite on the grounds of his Nova Scotia home.

again. Gardiner Hubbard died in December 1897. His National Geographic Society had been floundering. At the time of Hubbard's death, it had only one thousand members and was deeply in debt.[8]

The job of replacing Hubbard as National Geographic Society president fell into Bell's hands. The middle-aged inventor did not want to take the job.[9] But he later wrote in his diary that he felt he needed to become president of the society "in order to save it."[10]

He succeeded. Before Bell took over, the society's magazine was very dry and was read mainly by a small group of professors and scientists. To edit the magazine, Bell hired a young man named Gilbert Grosvenor, the son of a family friend.

Bell decided the magazine might be more popular if the writing were less technical. He also thought there should be more photographs of the faraway places described in the articles. These changes were made. Less than two years later, the society had gained seven hundred fifty new members.[11]

As the nineteenth century passed into the twentieth, Bell spent days and nights studying theories of flight with his kites. There was a happy occasion in the Bell family unrelated to work. Daughter Elsie had fallen in love with Gilbert Grosvenor. They were married in October 1900.

In August 1901, Helen Keller paid Bell a visit in Baddeck and lent him a hand with his test flights.

National Geographic Society and Exploration
The National Geographic Society has sponsored numerous expeditions to uncharted places around the world. The first took place in 1890 when a party of explorers journeyed to the mountain peaks on the Alaska-Canada border. The explorers were credited as the first people to see Canada's highest peak, Mount Logan, which reaches 19,524 feet above sea level. They named both a mountain and a glacier for society founder Gardiner Hubbard.

By then she was a beautiful and intelligent young student at Radcliffe College in Cambridge, Massachusetts.

Keller wrote of her trip to see Bell:

He had just constructed a boat that could be propelled by a kite with the wind in its favor, and one day he tried experiments to see if he could steer the kite against the wind. I was there and really helped him fly the kites. On one of them I noticed that the strings were of wire, and having had some experience in beadwork, I said I thought they would break. Dr. Bell said "No!" with great confidence, and the kite was sent up. It began to pull and tug, and lo, the wires broke, and off went the great red dragon, and poor Dr. Bell stood looking forlornly after it. After that he asked me if the strings were all right and changed them at once when I answered in the negative. Altogether we had great fun.[12]

On October 7, 1903, Samuel Langley planned to fly an airplane from his boat in the Potomac River.

It would be similar to the test he made for Bell a few years earlier. However, the airplane would have a pilot this time. He was a young engineer named Charles Manly. And this time Langley invited newspaper reporters to witness the event.

The plane took off from the boat and fell right into the water. Manly was not hurt, but the reporters on hand howled with laughter.

Langley tried again on December 8. Again, the plane took a nosedive into the water. Newspaper reporters called Langley a failure.

Langley never again made a serious effort to fly a manned airplane. Bell blamed the press. He later wrote, "The ridicule of the newspapers, however, effectively prevented Professor Langley from securing further financial aid, and, indeed, broke his heart."[13]

The Wright Brothers

Just nine days later, brothers Wilbur and Orville Wright succeeded where Langley and Bell had not. Orville flew the brothers' airplane above the sand dunes of Kitty Hawk, North Carolina, for twelve seconds on December 17, 1903. It was the first engine-powered manned flight of a heavier-than-air vehicle in history.

Was Bell happy for the Wrights, or was he jealous and angry? Some historians say he was pleased because the Wrights' flight was good for science. However, he did not show any reaction in the many letters he wrote soon afterward to friends and relatives.

Len Bruno, the curator of science manuscripts at the Library of Congress in Washington, D.C., said,

> You would think there would be some mention of manned flight in the letters he wrote in late 1903 or by the middle of 1904. But there's no mention of it in any letter to Langley or anyone else. We have no indication what his personal or professional reaction was.[14]

Perhaps Bell was making a statement by not acknowledging the Wrights' flight. However, his views on the flight will likely never be known.

Also in 1903, Mabel and Alexander Graham Bell celebrated the birth of their first grandchild. A boy was born to Elsie and Gilbert Grosvenor. He was named Melville Bell Grosvenor in honor of his great-uncle Melly. Shortly after the baby was born, Bell yelled into the baby's ear. The infant burst into tears. Bell called out excitedly, "He has perfect hearing!"[15]

Although the Wrights had achieved fame for being the first to fly, Bell thought their planes were not stable enough for practical use. The Wrights used two sets of wings, one over the other. Bell believed a style of kite made of triangular forms was the real future of successful flying. The complex form of triangles Bell used is called a tetrahedron. He thought adding a motor to a tetrahedral kite would support the weight of a man in the air.

Bell tested a number of different kites. He named many of them. The first was called *Oionos*, a Greek word meaning "bird of omen." In 1904 *Oionos* flew with the ease of a bird. In 1905 Bell built a kite he called *Frost King*. It was named after a friend named Walter Frost. *Frost King* was heavier and stronger than *Oionos*. It carried a pilot named Neil MacDermid about thirty feet into the air.[16] However, it did not have a motor as the Wright brothers' airplane did.

Bell's telephone days were in the distant past. It was by then nearly thirty years since he had made that extraordinary invention. Yet by 1905 there was no denying one fact: Bell's telephone was having an incredible impact on people's day-to-day lives. In that year there were 4 million telephones in the United States.[17]

Bell was lucky to have his father live to see most of his success and fame. But on August 7, 1905, Alexander Melville Bell died "quiet, and without struggle" at the age of eighty-six.[18]

This period of Bell's life was filled with family milestones. His younger daughter, Daisy, was married in 1905. Her husband was a government botanist named David Fairchild. In August 1906, Daisy and David gave Bell his second grandson, Alexander Graham Bell Fairchild. He would be called Sandy.

The same year, Bell's close friend Samuel Langley died. Bell was bitter about the way Langley had been treated by the newspapers. At Langley's funeral Bell gave a eulogy. He said, "His flying machine never had an opportunity of being fairly tried, [but] the man and his works will permanently endure."[19]

Bell refused to give up on his flying machines. He hired four men as assistants. One was Douglas McCurdy, the son of Bell's secretary. Another was Casey Baldwin, an engineering student. A third was Tom Selfridge, a young military officer. The fourth was Glenn Curtiss, a motorcycle maker from the upstate New York town of Hammondsport. The men were all young enough to be Bell's sons. In fact, Bell became close to them and treated them as if they were his sons.

Mabel became part of this group, too. She knew how much manned flight meant to her husband. She used her business sense to help the five men get the money they needed to keep their flight experiments going. She sold some property she had inherited in Washington. Then she suggested to her husband that the money be used to form an association, similar to the Volta Laboratory that had helped fund Bell's experiments with sound years earlier.

Aerial Experiment Association

Bell immediately accepted Mabel's generous offer. In 1907, the Aerial Experiment Association (AEA) was formed.

That same year the people of Baddeck began to see an unusual structure fronting the skyline around

Bell's house. To show that simple tetrahedral cells could be used to make an object of any shape, Bell built an eighty-foot-high tower made only of the cells.[20] To demonstrate how strong tetrahedral cells were, he and his friends and family often climbed it to enjoy the view from the top.

National Geographic marveled at Bell's creation that year. Alongside a photo feature showing the building of the tower, the magazine said,

> This considerable structure weighs less than 5 tons, and yet can carry a great weight. It is remarkable, not only for its strength and lightness, as well as cheapness, but also for the fact that it was put together in about 10 days by several unskilled laborers, and that every part of the work was done on the ground.[21]

On December 7, 1907, a group of onlookers showed up to see Bell's latest kite, *Cygnet*, fly. (A cygnet is a young swan.) The kite was made from 3,400 red silk-covered tetrahedrons.[22] Bell hoped it would carry young Tom Selfridge successfully into the air.

Cygnet was attached to a steamboat with a rope tow. As the boat took off and pulled the kite, it caught the wind and flew into the air. After a few minutes, the wind dropped off and *Cygnet* drifted downward. Unfortunately, the crew of the steamer in their excitement had forgotten to cut the towrope, and the kite was dragged in the water. Selfridge swam to safety, but the kite was ruined.

The opening ceremony for Bell's eighty-foot-high tetrahedral tower took place on August 31, 1907.

Aside from age, there was one other big difference between Bell and the other four men of the AEA. McCurdy, Baldwin, Selfridge, and Curtiss were all engineers. Bell was not. They steered Bell away from the tetrahedral design toward a biplane like the one the Wright brothers flew. Bell was influenced by their engineering backgrounds. He took their advice to build a motorized biplane.

On March 12, 1908, the men tested the AEA's first effort. Because its wings were covered with red silk, the biplane was called *Red Wing*. The test took place in Curtiss's hometown of Hammondsport, New York, instead of Baddeck. Spring came a bit earlier to Hammondsport than to Nova Scotia. Casey Baldwin was at the controls. Residents of Hammondsport showed up.

Red Wing and pilot Baldwin flew for a distance of 318 feet and 11 inches at about ten feet off the ground.[23] Since the Wright brothers had tested their aircraft in private, the flight of *Red Wing* was called "the first public flight in America."[24]

8

CONTINUING A LIFETIME OF INVENTION

Alexander Graham Bell loved kids. By 1908 he had several grandchildren. He let them and neighborhood youngsters help with his experiments. Once, some children gathered around him when he was working on a project. They began asking the busy inventor questions. One of his adult assistants tried to get the children to leave him alone.

Bell responded, "No, wait a minute. Let's never overlook the question of a child. Because a child looks at the world with an uncluttered mind."[1]

Bell was then in his early sixties. Many people at that age slow down and think about retiring. Bell, however, had too many ideas to consider slowing down. With his assistants, he built and tested more airplanes. One was called *White Wing*. It was so named because the men had run out of red silk and had used white cotton. *White Wing* flew five times in May 1908 before crashing on May 23.

In June 1908 the AEA flew another plane, called *June Bug*. *Silver Dart*, the AEA's next plane, flew both in Hammondsport and Baddeck. The men planned to fly it throughout that fall and winter.

By fall there was one less member of the AEA. The dangerous job of flight-testing had taken its toll on the group. Tom Selfridge was flying with Orville Wright in Virginia on September 17 when their

Alexander Graham Bell (center) is shown here with other members of the Aerial Experimentation Association (AEA).

plane crashed. Wright was seriously injured but survived. Selfridge died from his injuries.

When Douglas McCurdy flew *Silver Dart* for half a mile on February 23, 1909, it became the first time a vehicle heavier than air successfully flew in Canada.[2] On March 31, the AEA ceased to exist as a business. Its money had been used up, and its contract was finished. Glenn Curtiss left for Hammondsport to form his own aircraft company. McCurdy and Baldwin stayed with Bell to test airplanes for another year.

In spite of his success with biplanes, Bell did not completely give up on his dream of tetrahedral aircraft. He thought the biplane design had something to do with Selfridge's fatal accident. With Baldwin's help, Bell built two planes using the tetrahedral design. One was called *Cygnet II*. The other was called *Oionos*, the same name Bell had called one of his kites nearly ten years earlier.

Unlike the Wright brothers' biplanes, *Oionos* had three wings. It also had triangular prism units between the wings. However, neither *Cygnet II* nor *Oionos* flew. Both planes were too heavy to get off the ground.

Still, Alexander Graham Bell did not quit. He designed yet another tetrahedral airplane, which he called *Cygnet III*. This one did manage to fly, but just barely. It is estimated that *Cygnet III* traveled perhaps one foot in the air.

Aynsley MacFarlane, site manager of Alexander Graham Bell Historic Site in Baddeck, said it was typical for Bell to drop one project and go on to something new. She noted, "Very often he would set a goal, and once that goal was attained he would go on to something else. He wanted to get a tetrahedral airplane airborne and he did it."[3]

In 1910, Casey Baldwin and his wife, Kathleen, joined the Bells on the vacation of a lifetime. It was a cruise around the world that would last for months. Although Bell was much older than Baldwin, this trip showed how close the two families had become.

The Hydrofoil

By the next year, the Bells and the Baldwins were still touring the world. In Italy in 1911, Bell and Baldwin met an inventor who inspired them to take their work in a new direction. His name was Enrico Forlanini, and his invention was a boat called a hydrofoil.

Most boats displace water as they move. A hydrofoil uses thin blades positioned so that water striking them creates an effect similar to that of lift on an airplane's wings. There is high pressure below the blades and low pressure above them. This lifts the boat, and it moves while gliding on the surface of the water. It can travel at very high speeds.

Bell and Baldwin had dabbled a bit with hydrofoils before. However, they had looked at hydrofoils mainly as a means of helping airplanes take off from water. When Bell and Baldwin took a ride with Forlanini in one of his hydrofoils, they were as excited as children. They could not wait to get back to Canada to try to make their own hydrofoils to sell in North America.

The work on the hydrofoil completed a kind of circle for Bell. He had labored before on inventions to conquer sound, sickness, and the air. Now he would try to embark on his last frontier: the water.

Bell and Baldwin returned to Nova Scotia in the summer of 1911 and got right to work. Over the fall and winter months they designed and built their own hydrofoil, which they called a hydrodrome. They named it *HD-1*. It had short wings and a propeller

Bell experimented with hydrofoils in later life. One of his hydrofoils is seen here on Bras D'Or Lake in Nova Scotia.

that made it seem like a combined airplane and boat. Several times during the summer of 1912, they sailed it across a nearby lake. But in October it was damaged beyond repair in an accident.

Over the next two years they built three more hydrofoils. Their success was spotty. One public demonstration left the men embarrassed. While traveling on his yacht one day in 1913, the prince of Monaco sailed into Baddeck Bay. Bell invited the prince to watch a demonstration of their hydrofoil called *HD-3*. With the prince watching, *HD-3* took off and did a belly flop before turning over. The men discovered that the design of the hydrofoil's structure was flawed.

It was not structural problems, however, that put a stop to Bell and Baldwin's hydrofoil experiments in 1914. The halt was caused by events taking place three thousand miles away. World War I (1914–1918) broke out in Europe.

There were many reasons for the war, but basically they came down to long-standing hatred between peoples of different countries. On one side were Great Britain, France, Russia, and Serbia. On the other side were Germany, Turkey, Bulgaria, and Austria-Hungary. At first, the United States was neutral.

Bell felt the hydrofoil could have military uses. Since he was a citizen of the neutral United States, he felt uncomfortable designing and making any kind of possible war weapon. He decided instead to have the men working for him make pleasure boats to sell to area residents.

Though he was sixty-seven years old, Bell kept his busy schedule. He remained active in the AAPTSD. He continued to advise hearing-impaired people. He was no longer president of the National Geographic Society, but he still wrote articles for its magazine.

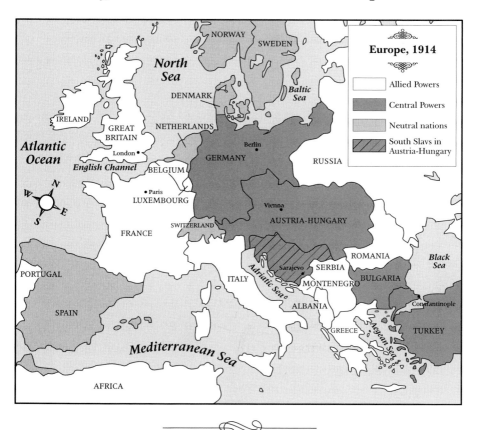

Bell considered the hydrofoil for possible military use after World War I broke out in Europe in 1914. This map shows how Europe was divided during the war.

It was Bell's interest in education that led him to work with a famous educator named Maria Montessori. She created the famous Montessori schools in the early 1900s. Her attitude was that children would learn more if they followed their own interests. That way, they would learn without realizing they were learning. Many people in Montessori's day thought her ideas were foolish or even dangerous. Alexander and Mabel Bell disagreed. They opened a Montessori school in part of their Washington home. They also opened one in Baddeck. Their grandchildren and the children of family friends attended these schools. The Bells became close friends with Montessori.

Few others were as enthusiastic as the Bells about Montessori's ideas. Those involved with standard educational methods did not support it. Also, the war in Europe made it difficult for Americans to stay in contact with Montessori headquarters in Italy. Excitement about the movement in North America faded within a couple of years, and Bell closed his schools.

No matter what Bell was working on at any moment, he was best known for one feat: the invention of the telephone. By 1915, the telephone company Bell had started was known as American Telephone & Telegraph Company (AT&T). Workers for AT&T had just finished erecting 130,000 telephone poles across the United States.[4] The country was finally connected by telephone wires from coast to coast.

Bell and Watson Together Again

Executives at AT&T thought it would be a great publicity stunt to have the two men who made the first telephone call in history make the first transcontinental telephone call, so they arranged a kind of reunion for Bell and Thomas Watson. Bell traveled to New York City. Watson went to San Francisco.

On January 25, 1915, Bell called Watson. The two spoke for twenty-three minutes. Near the end of the conversation, Bell paraphrased his famous line, "Mr. Watson, come here, I want to see you."

Watson responded, "Mr. Bell, I will, but it would take me a week now."[5]

That first transcontinental telephone call was a huge success. A song called "Hello Frisco, Hello" was written in its honor. It became the most popular song of 1915.[6]

In April 1917 the United States entered World War I. Bell offered his services to the United States government and the war effort. He was given a contract to build fourteen boats. However, he wanted government support to continue building his experimental hydrofoils. He believed hydrofoils could be used as submarine chasers. But the government was simply not interested in Bell's hydrofoils.

The war ended on November 11, 1918. Bell was seventy-one years old. He had gained weight and now suffered from diabetes, a life-threatening medical disorder. His age, weight, and medical condition, however, did not stop him from playing with his grandchildren and testing new inventions. Often the two pastimes were combined.

As she had done with her husband's airplane experiments years earlier, Mabel used her own money to help Bell build one more hydrofoil. He convinced the United States Navy to loan him two four-hundred-horsepower engines. With the war over, such surplus parts were easy to come by. The new hydrofoil was called *HD-4* and was completed in 1919. It was shaped like a torpedo and was the only full-sized hydrofoil Bell and Baldwin would make together.[7]

On September 9, 1919, Baldwin piloted the boat

to a world speedboat record of 70.86 miles per hour.[8] The record stood until 1963.[9] Still, the United States Navy was not interested in *HD-4*. Navy officials thought it would not be strong enough for action

Alexander Graham Bell and Mabel Hubbard Bell in Nova Scotia, 1909.

in a war. In the fall of 1921, the hydrofoil was taken apart and abandoned on the shore near Bell's mansion.

Despite the lack of interest in *HD-4*, Bell and Baldwin obtained a patent for it. It had taken years for the two men to convince the United States Patent Office that their hydrofoil had enough original features. A joint patent for *HD-4* was issued to Bell and Baldwin on March 28, 1922. On the same day, they received three more patents for features relating to operating or maintaining hydrofoils. These were Bell's last patents. They gave him a lifetime total of eighteen patents in his own name and twelve patents he shared with others.[10]

By the summer of 1922, diabetes had severely weakened Bell's body. He died on August 2. The funeral took place two days later. At the time of Bell's burial on August 4, the entire telephone system in North America was shut down for one minute as a tribute to its inventor.

An Unusual Funeral

In keeping with Bell's personality, Mabel refused to allow his funeral to be a somber event. Children romped as usual on the grounds of Bell's beloved Beinn Bhreagh. No one who attended wore traditional black mourning clothes. Instead, the women wore white and the men wore their typical summer clothes.

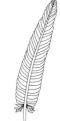

Alexander Graham Bell's funeral took place on August 4, 1922.

Bell was buried on the grounds of Beinn Bhreagh. His epitaph reads, "Inventor, Teacher, Born Edinburgh March 1847, Died a citizen of the USA, August 1922."[11]

Mabel Bell died five months later on January 3, 1923. She was buried next to her husband.

Shortly after the Bells' deaths, the tetrahedral tower was torn down. It had fallen into disrepair.

9

LEGACY

Most people—adults and children alike—think of Alexander Graham Bell only as the inventor of the telephone. Yet what was his greatest legacy? His great-grandson, Gilbert M. Grosvenor, said,

> I personally view Grampy Bell a little differently I guess than the average person on the street who thinks of him as the inventor of the telephone. I think of him as an educator of the deaf, someone who was profoundly interested in mainstreaming hearing-impaired people of all ages.[1]

Bell said so himself. In spite of all the time he spent inventing, as a young man Bell wrote, "Of one thing I become more sure every day—that my interest in the deaf is to be a life-long thing with me."[2]

For the rest of his life, Bell did not consider himself just an inventor. He listed his profession as "teacher of the deaf."[3]

Aynsley MacFarlane, site manager of Alexander Graham Bell National Historic Park in Baddeck, said,

> Although he never taught the deaf in a formal capacity after his Boston years, he was always involved in the instruction of the deaf. No matter what experimenting he would be doing, he'd always take the time to answer correspondence or help the deaf in some other way, especially the young. And he was constantly being contacted.[4]

Even Helen Keller, who had become a respected author and lecturer, dedicated her autobiography to Bell. She wrote, "To Alexander Graham Bell, who has taught the deaf to speak and enabled the listening ear to hear speech from the Atlantic to the Rockies, I dedicate this story of my life."[5]

Perhaps Bell's most enduring gift to the hearing-impaired was the American Association for the Promotion of the Teaching of Speech to the Deaf (AAPTSD). In 1956 its name was changed to the Alexander Graham Bell Association for the Deaf. It survives to this day, publishing books and journals, offering scholarships, supporting a library, and helping hearing-impaired people in many ways.

Of course, in his seventy-five years, Bell did much more than teach the deaf. He invented. According to Aynsley MacFarlane, aside from the

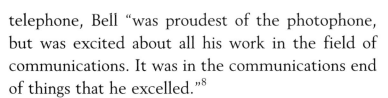

Hello or Ahoy?
Bell believed the telephone should be answered with the word *ahoy*. It was Thomas Edison who made up the word *hello*. Telephone historian Allen Koenigsberg notes that in the mid-1800s the word *hollo* was a slang expression for expressing surprise. Edison misspelled it as *hello*. Koenigsberg explains, "Given the nature of the circuits and the nature of the telephone receivers of the time, the word *hello* was good for carrying distances. Not all sounds carried well."[6] Koenigsberg wrote, "[I]magine—were it not for Edison's well known difficulty with spelling and hearing, we might all be answering callers today with 'Ahoy! Ahoy!' when the telephone rings."[7]

telephone, Bell "was proudest of the photophone, but was excited about all his work in the field of communications. It was in the communications end of things that he excelled."[8]

The photophone—which carried the human voice by a beam of light instead of over a wire—is the direct ancestor of today's popular cellular telephones.

Ahead of His Time

Many of Bell's other basic concepts and inventions served humankind years after his death. The idea of Bell's vacuum jacket was perfected into what is called an iron lung. It was used to aid victims of a disease called poliomyelitis, or polio. The iron lung helped many breathe during severe attacks of polio until a polio vaccine was developed in the early

1950s. Bell's bullet probe, which failed to help President Garfield, is considered by many to be the first step toward the development of the X-ray machine. The autograph telegraph Bell worked on in the 1870s is thought by some to be the forerunner of today's facsimile (fax) machine.

Bell's idea of tetrahedral construction in flight never really worked out. However, the tetrahedron has been used in tower and bridge construction. Although experts in the late 1910s and early 1920s shunned Bell's hydrofoil, engineers took another look at it in the years after World War II ended in 1945. They decided that Bell's idea had some merit. Today hydrofoils are used to provide ferry transportation in places such as Europe and Hawaii.

The National Geographic Society and its monthly magazine thrive today. A *National Geographic Magazine* editor named Charles McCarry wrote in 1988, "[E]very Editor since [Gilbert] Grosvenor has been guided by Bell's masterly instructions to be decisive and quick in sending people and cameras all over the world to bring back 'details of living interest beautifully illustrated by photographs.'"[9]

Bell might also be considered ahead of his time regarding education. The Montessori school system of teaching was generally rejected by educators in Bell's day. Today, it enjoys popularity as an alternative to standard forms of education.

Alexander Graham Bell is still remembered for his extraordinary dedication to invention and teaching.

Not all of Bell's ideas were successful. By today's standards, his promotion of visible speech might be seen as a failure. The visible speech system became known among the deaf as oralism. For a long time it was considered the official way for the deaf to communicate. However, many hearing-impaired people used Gallaudet's system of sign language in their homes. Over the last few decades, the hearing-impaired have adopted American Sign Language (ASL) as their preferred manner of communicating with each other.

Despite the failure of visible speech, it is hard to fathom the sheer number of Bell's ideas that were successful and how they continue to affect billions of people's lives so many years after his death.

CHRONOLOGY

1847—Born on March 3 in Edinburgh, Scotland.

1858—Makes wheat-husking machine, his first invention.

1862—Lives in London with grandfather.
–1863

1863—First teaching job, in Elgin, Scotland.

1864—Moves with family to London.

1867—Brother Ted dies of tuberculosis.

1870—Brother Melly dies of tuberculosis; Moves with family to Brantford, Ontario.

1871—Takes teaching job at Boston School for the Deaf.

1873—Takes job as professor of vocal physiology at Boston University.

1874—Meets Thomas Watson; Conceives idea of telephone while spending summer at family home in Brantford.

1876—Invents telephone; Presents it at Centennial Exhibition in Philadelphia.

1877—Marries Mabel Hubbard on July 11.

1878—Daughter Elsie May born on May 8.

1879—Defeats Elisha Gray and Western Union in court battle over patent; Moves with family to Washington, D.C.

1880—Experiments on photophone with Charles Sumner Tainter; Daughter Marian (Daisy) born on February 15.

1881—Invents bullet probe following shooting of President Garfield; Son Edward born and dies on August 15; Begins work on vacuum jacket.

1882—Becomes American citizen on November 10; Son Robert born and dies November 17.

1885—First visit to Nova Scotia.

1887—Meets Helen Keller.

1890—Founds American Association for the Promotion of the Teaching of Speech to the Deaf (AAPTSD); Moves to Baddeck, Nova Scotia.

1891—Begins flight experiments in Baddeck.

1893—Second home, Beinn Bhreagh, completed.

1897—Gardiner Hubbard dies.

1898—Becomes president of National Geographic Society; Starts kite experiments in Baddeck.

1902—Begins working with tetrahedrons.

1903—Wright brothers make history with first heavier-than-air manned flight in Kitty Hawk, North Carolina.

1905—Alexander Melville Bell dies on August 7.

1907—Forms Aerial Experiment Association (AEA) with four associates; Builds tetrahedral tower at his home in Nova Scotia.

1909—His airplane *Red Wing* makes first public flight in America.

1911—Starts working on hydrofoils with Casey Baldwin.

1915—In New York City, makes first transcontinental telephone call to Thomas Watson in San Francisco.

1919—Hydrofoil *HD-4* is piloted by Baldwin to world speedboat record.

1922—Dies on August 2.

CHAPTER NOTES

Chapter 1. "I Hear! I Hear!"

1. Helen Elmira Waite, *Make a Joyful Sound: The Romance of Mabel Hubbard and Alexander Graham Bell* (Philadelphia: Macrae Smith Company, 1961), pp. 129–132.

2. Ibid., p. 132.

3. *The American Experience*, "The Telephone," Simon & Goodman Picture Co. production, WGBH Educational Foundation, 1997.

4. Suzanne Hilton, *Here Today and Gone Tomorrow: The Story of World's Fairs and Expositions* (Philadelphia: The Westminster Press, 1978), p. 44.

5. Tony Foster, *The Sound and the Silence: The Private Lives of Mabel and Alexander Graham Bell* (Halifax, Nova Scotia: Nimbus Publishing, Ltd., 1996), p. 177.

6. Thomas B. Costain, *The Chord of Steel: The Story of the Invention of the Telephone* (Garden City, N.Y.: Doubleday & Company, Inc., 1960), p. 157.

7. *The American Experience*.

8. Waite, p. 137.

Chapter 2. Ghosts and Machines

1. Tony Foster, *The Sound and the Silence: The Private Lives of Mabel and Alexander Graham Bell* (Halifax, Nova Scotia: Nimbus Publishing, Ltd., 1996), p. 9.

2. Robert V. Bruce, *Bell: Alexander Graham Bell and the Conquest of Solitude* (Boston: Little, Brown and Company, 1973), p. 22.

3. Foster, p. 11.

4. Alexander Graham Bell, "Prehistoric Telephone Days," *National Geographic*, March 1922, pp. 239, 241.

5. Naomi Pasachoff, *Alexander Graham Bell: Making Connections* (New York: Oxford University Press, 1996), p. 16.

6. Bruce, p. 27.

7. Ibid., pp. 27–28.

8. Ibid., p. 34.

Chapter 3. Across the Waters

1. Alexander Graham Bell, "Prehistoric Telephone Days," *National Geographic*, March 1922, p. 228.

2. Tony Foster, *The Sound and the Silence: The Private Lives of Mabel and Alexander Graham Bell* (Halifax, Nova Scotia: Nimbus Publishing, Ltd., 1996), p. 78.

3. Ibid., p. 80.

4. Ibid.

5. Bell, p. 239.

6. Ibid.

7. Helen Elmira Waite, *Make a Joyful Sound: The Romance of Mabel Hubbard and Alexander Graham Bell* (Philadelphia: Macrae Smith Company, 1961), p. 69.

8. Personal interview with Brian Wood, October 22, 1997.

9. Ibid.

10. Ibid.

11. Ibid.

12. Personal interview with Brian Wood, June 10, 1998.

Chapter 4. Voice to Voice

1. Helen Elmira Waite, *Make a Joyful Sound: The Romance of Mabel Hubbard and Alexander Graham Bell* (Philadelphia: Macrae Smith Company, 1961), p. 80.

2. Personal interview with Tom Hutchinson, November 20, 1997.

3. Thomas A. Watson, *Exploring Life* (New York: D. Appleton and Company, 1926), p. 54.

4. Ibid., p. 59.

5. Personal interview with Brian Wood, November 21, 1997.

6. Watson, p. 63.

7. Personal interview with Tom Hutchinson, November 20, 1997.

8. Personal interview with Tom Hutchinson, November 24, 1997.

9. Robert V. Bruce, *Bell: Alexander Graham Bell and the Conquest of Solitude* (Boston: Little, Brown and Company, 1973), pp. 165–166.

10. Watson, p. 78.

11. Personal interview with Tom Hutchinson, November 20, 1997.

Chapter 5. A Baby Named Photophone?

1. *The American Experience*, "The Telephone," Simon & Goodman Picture Co. production, WGBH Educational Foundation, 1997.

2. Thomas A. Watson, *Exploring Life* (New York: D. Appleton and Company, 1926), p. 114.

3. Ibid.

4. Ibid., p. 115.

5. Ibid., pp. 121–122.

6. Roger Burlingame, *Out of Silence Into Sound: The Life of Alexander Graham Bell* (New York: The Macmillan Company, 1964), p. 81.

7. Helen Elmira Waite, *Make a Joyful Sound: The Romance of Mabel Hubbard and Alexander Graham Bell* (Philadelphia: Macrae Smith Company, 1961), p. 166.

8. Watson, pp. 151–152.

9. Ibid., p. 152.

10. *Biography*, "Alexander Graham Bell: Voice of Invention," Jaffe Productions in association with Actuality Productions, Inc., Arts and Entertainment Network, 1997.

11. Ibid.

12. Waite, p. 177.

Chapter 6. New Inventions, New Friends, New Scotland

1. Robert V. Bruce, "Alexander Graham Bell," *National Geographic*, September 1988, pp. 370–371.

2. Personal interview with Tom Hutchinson, November 24, 1997.

3. Bruce, p. 370.

4. Tony Foster, *The Sound and the Silence: The Private Lives of Mabel and Alexander Graham Bell* (Halifax, Nova Scotia: Nimbus Publishing, Ltd., 1996), p. 226.

5. Roger Burlingame, *Out of Silence Into Sound: The Life of Alexander Graham Bell* (New York: The Macmillan Company, 1964), p. 93.

6. Ibid.

7. Ibid.

8. Personal correspondence from Rachel Merritt, Mark Twain House, Hartford, Connecticut, December 10, 1997.

9. *The American Experience*, "The Telephone," Simon & Goodman Picture Co. production, WGBH Educational Foundation, 1997.

10. Ibid.

11. Personal interview with Tom Hutchinson, June 10, 1998.

12. Personal interview with Douglas Tarr, June 10, 1998.

13. Personal interview with Aynsley MacFarlane, December 23, 1997.

14. Helen Keller, *The Story of My Life* (Cutchogue, N.Y.: Buccaneer Books, 1976), p. 26.

15. Joseph P. Lash, *Helen and Teacher: The Story of Helen Keller and Anne Sullivan Macy* (New York: Delacorte Press, 1980), p. 43.

16. Keller, p. 34.

17. Robert V. Bruce, *Bell: Alexander Graham Bell and the Conquest of Solitude* (Boston: Little, Brown and Company, 1973), p. 401.

Chapter 7. Into the Air

1. Tony Foster, *The Sound and the Silence: The Private Lives of Mabel and Alexander Graham Bell* (Halifax, Nova Scotia: Nimbus Publishing, Ltd., 1996), p. 268.

2. Personal interview with Aynsley MacFarlane, December 23, 1997.

3. Robert V. Bruce, *Bell: Alexander Graham Bell and the Conquest of Solitude* (Boston: Little, Brown and Company, 1973), p. 301.

4. Helen Keller, *The Story of My Life* (Cutchogue, N.Y.: Buccaneer Books, 1976), p. 72.

5. Joseph P. Lash, *Helen and Teacher: The Story of Helen Keller and Anne Sullivan Macy* (New York: Delacorte Press, 1980), p. 176.

6. Jean Lesage, "Alexander Graham Bell Museum: Tribute to Genius," *National Geographic*, August 1956, p. 242.

7. Keller, p. 113.

8. Charles McCarry, "Three Men Who Made the Magazine," *National Geographic*, September 1988, p. 288.

9. Ibid.

10. Ibid.

11. Ibid., p. 291.

12. Keller, p. 218.

13. Alexander Graham Bell, "Aerial Locomotion," *National Geographic*, January 1907, p. 7.

14. Personal interview with Len Bruno, January 23, 1998.

15. Bruce, p. 427.

16. Ibid., p. 438.

17. Roger Burlingame, *Out of Silence Into Sound: The Life of Alexander Graham Bell* (New York: The Macmillan Company, 1964), p. 93.

18. Bruce, p. 422.

19. Ibid., p. 436.

20. *National Geographic*, "Dr. Bell's Tetrahedral Tower," October 1907, p. 672.

21. Ibid.

22. Foster, p. 316.

23. Lesage, p. 251.

24. Ibid.

Chapter 8. Continuing a Lifetime of Invention

1. *Biography*, "Alexander Graham Bell: Voice of Invention," Jaffe Productions in association with Actuality Productions, Inc., Arts and Entertainment Network, 1997.

2. Robert V. Bruce, *Bell: Alexander Graham Bell and the Conquest of Solitude* (Boston: Little, Brown and Company, 1973), p. 451.

3. Personal interview with Aynsley MacFarlane, January 7, 1998.

4. *The American Experience*, "The Telephone," Simon & Goodman Picture Co. production, WGBH Educational Foundation, 1997.

5. Ibid.

6. Ibid.

7. Personal interview with Aynsley MacFarlane, January 7, 1998.

8. Jean Lesage, "Alexander Graham Bell Museum: Tribute to Genius," *National Geographic*, August 1956, p. 255.

9. *Biography*.

10. Personal interview with Linda Fry, National Inventors Hall of Fame, Akron, Ohio, January 9, 1998.

11. Personal interview with Aynsley MacFarlane, January 9, 1998.

Chapter 9. Legacy

1. *Biography*, "Alexander Graham Bell: Voice of Invention," Jaffe Productions in association with Actuality Productions, Inc., Arts and Entertainment Network, 1997.

2. Robert V. Bruce, "Alexander Graham Bell," *National Geographic*, September 1988, p. 366.

3. Ibid.

4. Personal interview with Aynsley MacFarlane, January 9, 1998.

5. Helen Keller, *The Story of My Life* (Cutchogue, N.Y.: Buccaneer Books, 1976), p. 7.

6. Personal interview with Allen Koenigsberg, January 23, 1998.

7. Allen Koenigsberg, "The First 'Hello!': Thomas Edison, the Phonograph and the Telephone," *Antique Phonograph Monthly*, June 1987, p. 9.

8. Personal interview with Aynsley MacFarlane, January 9, 1998.

9. Charles McCarry, "Three Men Who Made the Magazine," *National Geographic*, September 1988, p. 287.

PLACES TO VISIT

Canada
Ontario
Bell Homestead, Brantford. (519) 756-6220. Bell's former home holds exhibits on the invention of the telephone. Next door is the Henderson House, Canada's first telephone business office. Open year round.

Nova Scotia
Alexander Graham Bell National Historic Site, Baddeck. (902) 295-2069. A large museum focuses on Bell's work and inventions in Nova Scotia, especially in aeronautics, hydrofoils, and with the deaf. Open year round.

United States
Massachusetts
Bell Atlantic Building, Boston. Bell's attic lab with original timbers, rafters, floorboards, and equipment is now in a room off the lobby. Open year round.

Washington, D.C.
Explorers Hall at the National Geographic Society. (202) 857-7588. Displays highlight the many expeditions sponsored by the society. Open year round.

National Air and Space Museum and National Museum of American History of the Smithsonian Institution. (202) 357-2700. Exhibits in the Air and Space Museum trace the history of flight. Displays on Bell's telephone are located in the National Museum of American History. Open year round.

GLOSSARY

assassin—A murderer of a politically important person.

autograph telegraph—An early name for a machine that would transmit a message in a person's actual handwriting.

autopsy—A medical examination done in order to determine the cause of death.

biplane—An airplane with two sets of wings at different levels.

caveat—A legal document stating that a person has a right to an invention in progress. Caveats are no longer used.

centennial—A one-hundredth anniversary.

hearing-impaired—Having less than normal hearing.

hydrofoil—A boat that moves by being lifted above, rather than cutting through, water.

lawsuit—A legal case accusing a person or company of wrongdoing.

multiple telegraph—A telegraph that can send more than one message at the same time.

patent—A document that states the name of the inventor and his or her invention.

pavilion—A building used to house exhibits.

phonautograph—An early machine that recorded on glass the vibrations created by the human voice.

photophone—An early wireless telephone.

professor—A teacher at a college or university.

sign language—A way of communicating with hand gestures.

telegraph—A machine that sends a message by way of electric pulses.

tetrahedron—A four-sided figure made up of triangles.

transcontinental—Across a continent.

tuberculosis—A bacterial illness that affects the lungs.

tutor—A private teacher.

vaccination—A method of preventing a person from getting a specific disease by exposing him or her to a weakened form of the disease.

visible speech—A special alphabet that includes a symbol for every sound the human voice is capable of making.

X ray—A photograph taken of the inside of a person's body.

FURTHER READING

Books

Bendik, Jeanne. *Eureka! It's a Telephone*. Brookfield, Conn.: Millbrook Press, 1993.

Dolan, Ellen M. *Thomas Alva Edison: Inventor*. Springfield, N.J.: Enslow Publishers, Inc., 1998.

Gutnik, Martin J. *Electricity: From Faraday to Solar Generators*. New York: Franklin Watts, 1986.

Keller, Helen. *The Story of My Life*. Cutchogue, N.Y.: Buccaneer Books, 1976.

McCormick, Anita Louise. *The Industrial Revolution in American History*. Springfield, N.J.: Enslow Publishers, Inc., 1998.

Moser, Barry. *Fly: A Brief History of Flight Illustrated*. New York: Willa Perlman Books, 1993.

Nahum, Andrew. *Flying Machines*. New York: Alfred A. Knopf, 1990.

St. George, Judith. *Dear Dr. Bell—Your friend, Helen Keller*. New York: Putnam's Sons, 1992.

Skurzynski, Gloria. *Get the Message: Telecommunications in Your High-Tech World*. New York: Bradbury Press, 1993.

Webb, Marcus. *Telephones: Words over Wires*. San Diego: Lucent Books, 1992.

Wepman, Dennis. *Helen Keller*. New York: Chelsea House, 1987.

Wilkinson, Philip, and Michael Pollard. *Scientists Who Changed the World*. New York: Chelsea House, 1994.

Internet Addresses

Alexander Graham Bell Association for the Deaf. 1996. <http://www.agbell.org> (July 13, 1998).

Alexander Graham Bell Institute. May 30, 1997. <http://bell.uccb.ns.ca> (July 13, 1998).

AT&T. "Who Was Alexander Graham Bell?" *BrainSpin.* 1997. <http://www.att.com/attlabs/brainspin/alexbell/teacher.html> (July 13, 1998).

National Geographic Society. *nationalgeographic.com.* 1998. <http://www.nationalgeographic.com> (July 13, 1998).

Pasadena Online. "Alexander Graham Bell Links." *Pasadena Kid's Page.* 1996. <http://www.e-znet.com/kids/AlexBellLinks.html> (July 13, 1998).

INDEX